Let's Stop the Fighting

A Biblical Approach
For Working Out Our Differences

Ricki Lee Brooks

Sound Communication

Let's Stop the Fighting
Published by Sound Communication
PO Box 4016
Silverdale, WA 98383
www.rickileebrooks.com

Most Scripture quotations are from HOLY BIBLE, NEW
INTERNAIONAL VERSION. Copyright © 1973, 1978, 1984
by International Bible Society.

Scripture quotations marked NASB are from the NEW AMERICAN
STANDARD BIBLE, Copyright © 1960, 1977
by the Lockman Foundation.

Scripture quotations marked NKJV are from the NEW KING
JAMES VERSION, Copyright © 1979, 1980, 1982
by Thomas Nelson, Inc. Nashville, TN

Scripture quotations marked LIVING BIBLE are from the The
LIVING BIBLE, Copyright © 1971
by Tyndale House Publishers. Carol Stream, IL

ISBN-13: 978-0615644592

Contents

Preface

The concept referred to as Irreconcilable Differences hangs heavy in the air today. Marriages are falling apart at ever accelerating rates. Families divide at the drop of an unkind word. Business partners fold entire companies on account of their personal differences. Friendships fade for lack of knowledge in the negotiation department. Political parties once united, now face division in the ranks. Walking away has taken the leading role. Walking together plays a bit part.

But wait, lest we Christians place our thumbs behind our lapels and stick our chests out to the crowd, let's remind ourselves that the divorce rate within the Church is just as high as without. Let's be reminded that church splits have been responsible for a whole new genre of humor: it's called the church joke...

...Have you heard about the new church doll? Yeah, you wind it up and watch it do the splits.

Pathetic, yet too close to reality for us to ignore.

Jesus said...
A new command I give you: Love one another. As I loved you, so you must love one another. By this all men will know that you are my disciples, if you love one another (John13:34,35 NIV).

What a command! What a hope! But where do we start?

We start with God's revelation. If we are correctly related to God through a saving knowledge and dependence upon Jesus Christ then we are required to draw our data from The Book—the Bible. In it is all we need for ordering our lives. Throughout its God-breathed pages are truths intended for our transformation. Learning them, heeding them and doing them will produce spiritual fruit. So, let's get started.

A note from Ricki

My wife, Vanita, and I spent every day together in ministry. During the course of that ministry we quite often were confronted with conflict within the Church. At first we read several books on conflict resolution from a management-theory point of view. Then, like all believers should, we began to pour over the Bible. We needed to know if God's way was different since we wanted very much for God's family to live in harmony. As we studied, we began to write. This book, along with a commentary on Paul's Letter to the Philippians and an expanded capacity for coaching others, is one of the results. However, in March of 1999, a drunk driver took Vanita's life. Needless to say, I put several things aside at that time. One of them was the completion of this manuscript. A few years later conflict reared its ugly head in the church I now serve. When it did, I thought long and hard about how gifted Vanita was at implementing biblical principles for conflict resolution. I knew then the manuscript needed some final editorial work so that it might serve the purposes for which she longed—that God's people could learn about both the need for unity within the Body of Christ and how to implement unity within the Body of Christ. So, if you find this study helpful, thank our Lord Jesus—the One to whom Vanita would have directed all the credit.

Praying for Conflict Resolution

Jesus Told Us Why: John 17
Paul Told the Church Ladies How: Philippians 4:2-7

We recently read about an exasperated mom who sent her disobedient little boy to his room. When his time was up, he came out far more confident than when he had been sent in.

He said, "I've been thinking about what I did and I said a prayer to God."

"That's fine," his mother said, "if you ask God to make you good, he will help you."

"Oh, I didn't ask him to help me be good," the little fella replied. "I asked him to help you put up with me."

We found that little gem by reading through a list of quotes and anecdotes. Here's another…

It seems a little guy was attending church with his family when a flash of insight concerning prayer and conflict resolution suddenly came over him. Here's how the storyteller related the incident (and if it's just a tall tale rather than real history, we're still a little richer for it):

"We watched an especially verbal and boisterous child being hurried out, slung under his irate father's arm. No one in the congregation so much as raised an eyebrow—

until the child captured everyone's attention by crying out in a charming southern accent, 'Ya'll pray for me now!'"

We can laugh because we totally get it.

It seems all of us want to pray, "God there's some conflict here! Help me get the best of it!"

It makes sense since the requests are coming from the hearts of children. However, what often makes sense for children should not be so sensible for mature adults. Instead, we will be far better served if we listen to the advice of two other selections we found in the same list…

First, William Law said, "There is nothing that makes us love a man so much as prayer for him." One has to wonder, "Why doesn't that choice bit of wisdom not pop up more often when people are held in the tight clutches of conflict?"

Second, President Lincoln said, "I have been driven many times to my knees by the overwhelming conviction that I had nowhere else to go. My own wisdom, and that of all about me seemed insufficient for the day." Considering the greatness of this hero and the enormity of the conflict he faced, once again, we need to ask, "Why are more of us not following his example?"

It seems logical. We could and should. However, like the children in the above anecdotes and unlike the advice in the quotes from Mr. Law and Mr. Lincoln, most people, if they think to pray at all during times of conflict, pray for themselves. They pray for victory. They pray for advantage. The Bible leads us another direction.

So how should we pray when faced with conflict? Well, in a few moments, we'll get some real nitty-gritty and moment by moment advice as we investigate the conflict resolution model the Apostle Paul gave the two church ladies, Euodia and Syntyche, in Philippians 4:2-7. However, before that, let's first consider why we should pray for conflict resolution.

Why We Should Pray For Conflict Resolution

Where better to look for an answer to the why question than the Lord Jesus himself. In chapter seventeen of his gospel, the Apostle John recorded the words of Jesus when the Lord prayed to the Father in anticipation of the crucifixion. Notice a part of what he prayed (John 17:13-15 NIV):

I am coming to you now, but I say these things while I am still in the world, so that they may have the full measure of my joy within them. I have given them your word and the world has hated them, for they are not of the world any more than I am of the world. My prayer is not that you take them out of the world but that you protect them from the evil one.

Did you pay attention? Look at the last two sentences again: *I have given them your word and the world has hated them, for they are not of the world any more than I am of the world. My prayer is not that you take them out*

of the world but that you protect them from the evil one.
Praying on behalf of the apostles, Jesus said the world
would hate them. Yet, he did not ask that they be
removed from that hatred. He did not ask God to knock-
out those who would generate and extend that hatred.
Instead, he simply prayed they be protected from the evil
one. In the face of hatred and conflict, Jesus simply
wanted the apostles to avoid giving in to Satan.

If this were the end of his prayer it would be sufficient,
but there is more. What Jesus desired for the apostles, he
wants for all believers. In verse twenty, Jesus prayed, *My
prayer is not for them alone. I pray also for those who
will believe in me through their message.* Jesus prayed for
us! And he did not finish with this. He went on. So, let's
see where his prayer went (John 17:20-23 NIV):

*My prayer is not for them alone. I pray also for those
who will believe in me through their message, that all of
them may be one, Father, just as you are in me and I am
in you. May they also be in us so that the world may
believe that you have sent me. I have given them the glory
that you gave me, that they may be one as we are one: I
in them and you in me. May they be brought to complete
unity to let the world know that you sent me and have
loved them even as you have loved me.*

When Jesus prayed for us, he prayed specifically that we
be a people united, not divided. In fact, his words were
quite explicit: *May they be brought to complete unity.* But
why? The answer came in his next breath: *to let the world
know that you sent me and have loved them even as you*

have loved me. The product of unity is what Francis Schaeffer called "The Final Apologetic." In his book, "The Mark of the Christian," Schaeffer argued that the best form of evangelism was for Christians to get along. His point must not go unheeded: continual, persistent, unresolved conflict between Christians has the exact opposite impact on the world from what God desires. Here's part of what Schaeffer wrote, "...we cannot expect the world to believe that the Father sent the Son, that Jesus' claims are true, and that Christianity is true, unless the world sees some reality of the oneness of true Christians."* This is exactly why Jesus prayed as he did. The Lord indicated that two things would occur as a result of Christian unity: first, unbelievers would believe our claims that God the Father sent God the Son; and, second, unbelievers would believe that God the Father loves us as much as he loves his One and Only Son.

Now if this is true, the opposite is also true. If we allow conflict to divide us, if we allow disunity to be the hallmark of who we are, the world will not believe God the Father sent God the Son and the world will not believe that God loves us. They will be wrong, but they will have arrived at a reasonable conclusion. It will be reasonable to them, because we—through our lack of agenda harmony—will have given them every reason to

---

*Schaeffer, F.A. The Mark of a Christian: Vol. 4 of "The Complete Works of Francis A. Schaeffer, A Christian Worldview." Crossway Books; Westchester, Illinois; 1982, p. 189.

believe just the opposite of the truth. If and when we allow conflict to tear at us and to tear us apart, we also destroy our effectiveness as ambassadors for Christ.

Just what does this teach us about prayer and conflict resolution? Well, at the very least, it teaches us that whenever we face conflict our motivation to pray should stem from a hope that in all we say and do we will not destroy our testimony. Two things, therefore, stand out: we should pray that everyone involved with the conflict will be protected from the evil one; and we should pray that unity will be of greater value to everyone involved than our personal differences.

Think about it. You are faced with conflict. You now have a choice:

•   You can react without thinking. If you do, you will not pray. You will engage your opponent in your own strength. When you do, you will be susceptible to the evil one...and your conflict may very well blow up in your face. Your testimony will be damaged. If there are unbelievers involved or observing, you will jeopardize their opportunity for seeing the truth about God.

•   You can wait to respond. If you do, you may think to pray. When you pray, you can ask God to protect you from the influence of the evil one. You can ask God to help you value your relationship more than the issue causing conflict. And you can ask God to help you negotiate this conflict in a way that maintains the power of your testimony.

Think about it. How would this change patterns between a husband and wife? How would this alter the many disputes found within church congregations? How would this impact negotiations between co-workers? How would this counter the tension between management and labor? That's motivation.

How We Should Pray For Conflict Resolution

Now how do we take this motivation to pray for conflict resolution and translate it into everyday practice? Well for that, let's get to the Church Ladies. Their names are Euodia and Syntyche. They can be found in Philippians 4:2-7 (NIV). Here's what the Apostle Paul wrote:

I plead with Euodia and I plead with Syntyche to agree with each other in the Lord. Yes, and I ask you, loyal yokefellow, help these women who have contended at my side in the cause of the gospel, along with Clement and the rest of my fellow workers, whose names are in the book of life. Rejoice in the Lord always. I will say it again: Rejoice! Let your gentleness be evident to all. The Lord is near. Do not be anxious about anything, but in everything, by prayer and petition, with thanksgiving, present your requests to God. And the peace of God, which transcends all understanding, will guard your hearts and your minds in Christ Jesus.

At this point a little background information is necessary.

First, the Church in Philippi was a strong church. Paul had some great things to say about them. He said they were his partners in spreading the life-changing message of Jesus Christ (1:3-5). He thanked them for financially investing in the ministry of his missionary journeys (4:10-14). He also indicated that there were times when they alone supported his work when no other churches would share the burden (4:15,16).

Second, even though they were a great church, they were not perfect. Problems had infiltrated the church. And, while we cannot be entirely sure what those problems were, we do know that Paul was concerned enough to write to the church about the need for unity, agenda harmony, and conflict resolution. In his opening prayer he prayed they would be able to know what was really important (1:9,10). He urged them to be like-minded, one in spirit, and one in purpose (2:1-4). He told them they needed to develop an attitude like that of Jesus: personal humility rather than personal pride (2:5-11). And he asked them to work out their problems without bickering, complaining, arguing, or murmuring (2:12-18).

Throughout his letter to the Church in Philippi, Paul provided many principles for building great relationships and resolving conflict. As he started to wind things down, he addressed the two church ladies and their problem. Apparently, their conflict—if not at the heart of the Philippian problem—weighed on his heart enough to prompt his direct intervention. In the process, the Spirit of God used Paul to teach the Philippians five lessons on how to change their behavior before interpersonal problems threatened to do long-term damage. The first four dealt with how people should respond to one another in the middle of conflict. The fifth dealt with how people should pray in the middle of conflict crisis. Let's look quickly at the first four before we develop the fifth.

The first lesson came as he wrote *I plead with Euodia and I plead with Syntyche to agree with each other in the Lord.* The little phrase *agree with each other in the Lord* is translated by J.B. Phillips in The New Testament in Modern English as *to make up your differences as Christians should.* This clearly renders the meaning of Paul's plea. If the church ladies were going to get past their conflict they would have to work through their differences for the sake of their devotion to the Lord Jesus Christ. This demands that true Christian character win out over pride.

The second lesson followed immediately as Paul wrote: *Yes, and I ask you, loyal yokefellow, help these women who have contended at my side in the cause of the gospel, along with Clement and the rest of my fellow workers, whose names are in the book of life.* Paul recognized that Euodia and Syntyche might need some help with their conflict resolution, so he called upon someone he referred to as his *loyal yokefellow* to help them.

The third lesson is found in the next two sentences: *Rejoice in the Lord always. I will say it again: Rejoice!* Paul wanted the church ladies to remember their common roots. So smack in the middle of this whole thing he reminded them about the need to rejoice in the Lord. While they may have been in no particular mood to celebrate one another, they could take joy in their relationship to Jesus Christ. Paul wanted them to see that it should come as no surprise that neither of them was perfect. Problems could be expected. They <u>had</u> been in need of a Savior after all.

The fourth lesson had to do with being gracious. Paul wrote: *Let your gentleness be evident to all. The Lord is near.* The Greek word behind *gentleness* has also been translated accurately as considerateness, magnanimity, fairness, forbearance, and even graciousness. Consider the definitions for the first two:

<u>Considerateness:</u> thoughtfulness concerning the rights and feelings of others.

<u>Magnanimity:</u> loftiness of spirit enabling one to bear trouble calmly, to disdain meanness and revenge, and to make sacrifices for worthy ends.

The point could not be more clear: instead of fighting, Euodia and Syntyche needed to exhibit *gentleness* to one another. Anything less exposed them to corporate failure.

Having given Euodia, Syntyche, the Loyal Yokefellow, and the entire church four valuable lessons on how to behave toward one another in the middle of conflict, Paul turned his attention to prayer. In essence he wanted them to know that if their behavior was going to rise above personal differences they would need to trust God about everything—including one another and one another's issues. Here's what he wrote:

Do not be anxious about anything, but in everything, by prayer and petition, with thanksgiving, present your requests to God. And the peace of God, which transcends all understanding, will guard your hearts and your minds in Christ Jesus

How is it that Paul could command people involved with interpersonal conflict *to not be anxious about anything*? How is such a thing even possible? Are we supposed to be able to turn our emotions on and off at a whim? The answer came in what Paul wrote next: *but in everything, by prayer and petition, with thanksgiving, present your requests to God.* Paul could tell them not to be anxious, because he knew—should they choose to take the option—that they possessed immediate access to God through prayer…and God could certainly calm their troubled hearts.

Now stop for a moment. Do not take this for granted. This is not Christianity 101. This is not simple religion. Instead, this is an all out, in your face reality check on the nature of our relationship with God. Does he or does he not have the ability to help us with our conflicts? Will he go before us or will he leave us with our own feeble abilities? Can he…will he change our attitudes or are we doomed to live with the anxiety we experience in the middle of conflict?

The Apostle Paul had no doubt about this. He wanted Euodia and Syntyche to have no doubts. And, of course, through the words of the Apostle Paul, God is teaching us that we should have no doubts. Face conflict with prayer.

Still, we can ask how. How should we pray when faced with conflict? Well, consider the very words Paul used when talking about our conversation with God:

Prayer: a general term for talking with God

Petition: a general term for asking something of God

Thanksgiving: that which demonstrates our awareness of and gratefulness for God's love and good-will toward us

Requests: the specific items of our petitions

These words describe and define a true conversation with God. They have nothing to do with repetitive rituals. They have nothing to do with some crazy form of wish fulfillment. Instead, they describe and define honest interaction between us and the one who created us. He is a person. We are persons. He is relational. We are relational. He is large and in charge. We are not. He can change hearts. We need him to change ours.

However, Paul had specific intentions when he wrote: *Do not be anxious about anything, but in everything, by prayer and petition, with thanksgiving, present your requests to God. And the peace of God, which transcends all understanding, will guard your hearts and your minds in Christ Jesus.* To what anxiety was Paul referring? The context makes it clear: the anxiety that existed within Euodia and Syntyche—and probably the entire church—on account of their personal squabbles. So what would be the primary focus of these prayer efforts? The answer is not too difficult. In fact, let's flesh it out by putting some words in the Apostle's mouth:

"Euodia, instead of being anxious where Syntyche is concerned, would you please pray about your situation with her? And, Syntyche, I need to ask the same of you. Ladies, talk to God about your problem before you talk to others. In fact, talk to God before you talk with one another. And don't just talk to him…get specific. Ask God to help you have the mind of Christ, to be loving, and to be done with pride (lesson #1). Ask him for a third party to mediate the trouble between you and your one time coworker (lesson #2). Ask God to keep Jesus on your mind. If you cannot find joy in one another right now, let your joy in Christ rule all that you do and all that you say (lesson #3). Ask him for the strength to be gentle with one another, to forbear with one another, to be gracious with one another (lesson #4). Ask God to ease your anxiety. And don't stop with your petitions, remember to give thanks. Syntyche, surely there is much that you can thank God about concerning Euodia. Euodia, the same applies to you where Syntyche is concerned. Thank God for the ministry you accomplished together in the past. Thank God he saw fit to save the other person from her sins. Thank God he created her in his image. Thank God your sister in Christ will inherit all the blessings of heaven. Ladies, if you will pray about your situation, if you will give thanks for one another, then the peace of God will prevent you from making matters worse. He will guard your hearts. He will give you peace where you thought you would only know anxiety."

Can you imagine what might have happened to the conflict resolution process if both the church ladies followed through on this kind of prayer? Can you imagine what will happen if you and those you relate to determine to pray like this if and when you are faced with yet another conflict?

Think about it. The ragged edge that usually accompanies conflict will be smoothed out when we determine to pray for our conflict partner rather than protesting against his or her opinions, comments, and/or actions.

Think about it. The goal of getting back on track with a conflict partner will arrive much sooner if we determine to talk with God about our situation before we go off talking to others.

Think about it. If we break this down even further, how much better would agenda harmony be if we went even deeper in our prayers and began to thank God for the good things we know to be true about our conflict partner before we began fixating on his or her problems?

Well, Paul made it quite clear how much better it could be when he wrote, *And the peace of God, which transcends all understanding, will guard your hearts and your minds in Christ Jesus.* Where conflict gains traction between two or more people, it can be replaced by true peace. Where anxiety rules the hearts and minds of those involved with conflict, it can be replaced by the *peace of God* to guard those hearts and minds.

Asking God for help can facilitate rapid and powerful healing in conflict situations. Troubled relationships can be mended. They can rediscover harmony since peace in a relationship marks the decline of insecurities and the increase of trust and loyalty. There may well be some differences, but those differences never need to become wedges of separation. When we pray we do not redirect God, we redirect ourselves. We center ourselves in God's love (not our pride). We focus ourselves on God's glory (not our egos). We accommodate ourselves to God's will (not our desires). We mobilize ourselves for God's mission (not our agendas). We equip ourselves with God's word (not our opinions). We keep ourselves in God's providence (not our carelessness).

On the other hand, reacting to conflict without God's help can escalate the problem. We may move from an uneasy feeling to pinpointing one or more faults in another. If we let ourselves get sucked in, we'll begin to focus on the person rather than the issue. Once this occurs, it becomes a contest we feel we must win. If we do not, it means we were wrong and the other person is vindicated. Now we can't have that, can we? In order to win we resort to undermining the other person's character. All the while our conflict partner has probably been going through the same process of escalation.

Next, we each begin the process of saving face. We begin to protect ourselves by forming alliances. We need to rope others in as though sheer numbers will demonstrate the depth of "bad and wrong" in the person with whom we're experiencing conflict. We also need to split the other person's alliances. So we go out of our way to establish ties to his or her "teammates" in order to erode any popular support he or she may possess. Finally, since the other person will simply not relent or repent, we determine they are unworthy and, therefore, must be let go. Good bye. Good riddance. Give up.

The relationship is finally destroyed. Both our conflict partner and we are greatly diminished. We will move forward in life, but the scars will never go away. Suspicion will now invade most of our relationships. Trust will always be just a little harder to come by. Giving loyalty will be an uneasy proposition. As children of God, our faith will be hampered and our desire to give God public credit will wane. If this unresolved conflict involved a group of people, the organization will be damaged and discredited. Like an individual, it may continue, but its banner will never be quite so clean. Its corporate memory will be cloudy. Its present members will walk on egg-shells. Its guests and new members will sense that something is not quite right. In the end, this scenario will be tragic. It does not need to be like this.

If we will simply pray, we will give ourselves a huge advantage in resolving conflict. We can move on from there, but there is where we must start.

Application

Reading Step

Please read through John 17 and Paul's Letter to the Philippians. Now read them again two or three more times. Yup, that's right. Read for memory.

Thinking Step

Martin Luther's scribe, Veit Dietrich, said of him: "No day passes that he does not give three hours to prayer..." And when asked what he would be doing the next day, Luther said, "Work, work, from early to late. In fact, I have so much to do that I shall spend the first three hours in prayer."

Think about that for a moment. Luther believed that without much prayer the work he involved himself with would become futile. On the other hand, most people think there is so much to do they neglect to spend time in prayer. This seems to be especially true with conflict.

Here's the way it works. Something happens. Conflict erupts...and we feel the urgency to "fix" the problem immediately. Usually that means talking. Words just seem to start flowing...

"He said…"

"She said…"

"Did not…"

"Did too…"

Seldom do we take the time to ask God for help before we begin the talking process. As a result, we usually stumble and mumble our way through. Sometimes it works. Sometimes it does not. We have to wonder, how much would we increase our odds for success if we followed Luther's example? The answer is obvious: the odds would get better and better.

For example, notice the following passages of Scripture:

1.   Genesis 18

When faced with a great problem, what did Abraham do?

2.   Exodus 33:12-23

When uncertain, what did Moses do?

3.   Matthew 26:36-42

When overwhelmed with sorrow, what did Jesus do?

Now we are not saying God will speak to you audibly. We are not saying you will receive a definitive and immediate answer. We are not saying God will appear and take away all your troubles. The Bible does not promise such things. What we are promised is this:

All Scripture is God-breathed and is useful for teaching, rebuking, correcting and training in righteousness, so that the man of God may be thoroughly equipped for every good work (2 Timothy 3:16,17 NIV);

and this,

Blessed is the man who does not walk in the counsel of the wicked or stand in the way of sinners or sit in the seat of mockers. But his delight is in the law of the LORD, and on his law he meditates day and night (Psalm 1:1,2 NIV);

and this,

Jesus, as he prepared his disciples for his departure, said, *I have much more to say to you, more than you can now bear. But when he, the Spirit of truth comes, he will guide you into all truth. He will not speak on his own; he will speak only what he hears, and he will tell you what is yet to come* (John 16:12,13 NIV);

and this from the Apostle James,

If any of you lacks wisdom, he should ask God, who gives generously to all without finding fault, and it will be given to him. But when he asks, he must believe and not doubt, because he who doubts is like a wave of the sea, blown and tossed by the wind (James 1:5,6 NIV).

28

You see, when the Word of God is read, studied, and learned, then the Holy Spirit of God will remind the child of God about the truth of God which will then lead to attitudes and behaviors that resemble those belonging to the Son of God and which ultimately please God the Father. So, okay, we recognize this is quite a mouthful, but read it again (slowly) and think about it:

when the Word of God is read, studied, and learned

then the Holy Spirit of God will remind the child of God

about the truth of God
>which will then lead to attitudes and behaviors
>that resemble those belonging to the Son of God

>and which ultimately please our Father God.

So,
>if you love God a great deal...

>if you know the Bible well...

>if you pray for every circumstance...

then you will have the Holy Spirit reminding you of truth and leading you into an ever closer walk with God.

Moving Out Step

May we ask you to memorize four things? Here they are, neat and simple...

1. Based on John 17: We should pray that everyone involved with conflict will be protected from the evil one.

2. Based on John 17: We should pray that unity and harmony within our relationships will be of greater value to everyone involved in a particular conflict than their personal differences.

3. Based on Philippians 4:2-7: We should pray for those with whom we experience conflict.

4. Based on Philippians 4:2-7: We should always find something to thank God about concerning those with whom we experience conflict.

Finally, it will not be enough to simply remember these instructions about prayer. Begin to practice them.

Principles for Conflict Resolution

From the Apostle Paul's Letter to a
Successful, Yet Troubled Church: Philippians

She was just fifteen. Tears filled her eyes and quivers moved her lips. She pressed her hands over her ears. Her mother's shouts exploded her emotions and her restraint. Suddenly, she screamed, "SHUT UP! JUST SHUT UP!"

Conflict.

From all accounts, he stood above the rest. His preaching touched hearts and informed minds. His church suffered growth pains. People came from all around to follow his leadership. Quietly, however, on one otherwise normal morning, his wife walked out. She did not come back. He resigned. They divorced. Their children cringed. The church almost fell apart. The community laughed.

Conflict.

Across the table he stared into the other man's eyes. Slowly, deliberately, he stood up. Pointing his finger at his new adversary's face, he said, "Never, never, never have we done it like that before." It was classic. The obstruction grew from long years of control and power. How dare anyone else presume to offer guidance for his small organization?

Conflict.

The meeting was informal. Few were invited. She figured the privacy of her own home served to strengthen her cause. Slowly she began. "I've been studying my Bible at great length lately. I've discovered something our church has never taught before. Now I'm wondering if our Pastor is really the man to lead us."

Conflict.

8:30pm. Once again, he failed to come home on time. Even the children wondered why Daddy seemed to be away so much. There were those strange phone calls. The phone would ring. The Mrs. would answer, "Hello." Click. Nothing. The caller hung up. And what about those new clothes he seemed to be buying so quickly over the past few weeks. Why the change in style? And what of his quiet, pensive demeanor of late? Did she detect a note of guilt sketched in his eyes? Finally, the day came. He said, "We need to talk..."

Conflict.

Ring. Ring. "ABC Products. This is Sam Johnson. How can I help you?"

"Mr. Johnson, my name is Jane Smith. I work in accounts receivable for XYZ Industries. I'm calling to find out when we can expect payment on your overdue account. I see that ABC Products has been issued two past-due notices."

Silence.

"Mr. Johnson? Mr. Johnson are you still there?"

"Ah, yes, sorry. You seem to have caught me off guard. I was under the impression that bill had been paid. Let me check with my partner and I'll call you back."

"Well, okay, Mr Johnson. What time will you be calling?"

"Ah, well, I'm not really sure. I'll call you soon. Goodbye." Click. Sam's mind began to race, *"Not another one. What is George doing? He knows the books are his responsibility. I know there has been plenty of income to cover our expenses. Why are these bills not being paid?"*

Conflict.

Not one of the above scenarios is false. Unfortunately, they are also not unusual. They could be the stories of people you know—right there in your family, your community, your church, your business. Conflict is all around us. Unfortunately, many of us do not know how to resolve the conflict we face. It's been the same since Adam and Eve bit the forbidden fruit. However, we do not have to settle for unresolved conflict.

We have the distinct advantage of studying the Bible— God's Word—to find answers and methods for resolving conflict. So, grab your Bible again. Open it to the New Testament book called Philippians. As you will recall from our last chapter, it's a little letter the Apostle Paul wrote to the church in the ancient city of Philippi.

It was a church that contributed greatly to the missionary work of the Apostle Paul and his missionary team (1:3-6; 4:10-19). It was also a church with the same potential for conflict as faced by modern man. In fact, as we noted in the last chapter, the Church of Philippi suffered some form of conflict that seemed to stem from a disagreement between two of Paul's former helpers—Euodia and Syntyche (4:2,3). We're not really sure just what that conflict involved. However, from the flow of the letter we know trouble was either underway or near to eruption.

In Philippians 1, Paul used himself as an example as he told them of his own conflict (1:15-18). In Philippians 2, he implored them to do nothing out of selfishness, but instead to take upon themselves the nature of Jesus Christ which is marked by servanthood and humility (2:1-11). In Philippians 3, Paul urged the Philippian believers to forsake interest in themselves for confidence in Christ (3:7-11). Finally, in Philippians 4, he dealt specifically with the trouble brewing between Euodia and Syntyche (4:2-9).

Once again, the insight we gain from this letter can help us greatly in our own struggles to become better managers of conflict. Specifically in Philippians 2:12-18, we will find several principles upon which we might build both a Christ and principle centered approach to conflict resolution.

Let's begin then with a simple theme...

If we desire to build solid relationships we need to understand and accept some principles for working out our differences.

The Apostle Paul wrote,

Therefore, my beloved, as you have always obeyed, not as in my presence only, but now much more in my absence, work out your own salvation with fear and trembling, for it is God who works in you both to will and to do for His good pleasure. Do all things without complaining and disputing, that you may become blameless and harmless, children of God without fault in the midst of a crooked and perverse generation, among whom you shine as lights in the world, holding fast the word of life, so that I may rejoice in the day of Christ that I have not run in vain or labored in vain. Yes, and if I am being poured out as a drink offering on the sacrifice and service of your faith, I am glad and rejoice with you all. For the same reason you also be glad and rejoice with me.

Philippians 2:12-18 (NKJV)

In this brief passage, Paul has turned his attention to the need within the Philippian Church for rising above personal differences. For one reason or another there had been ongoing difficulty which gave rise to *complaining and disputing.* This in-fighting could never serve the purpose of creating and maintaining a church beautiful enough to be a witness for Jesus Christ in the *midst of a crooked and perverse generation.*

The answer then for differences is not fighting. Neither is

it to cover them or hide them. Rather differences should be mutually worked out until a sound resolution is found. The principles that follow will draw this out in more detail. The beauty of it all is this: these principles are trans-cultural. They apply to the church, the marriage, the family, and any other relational organization. They were applicable in the first century and they are applicable today. They will work in the East and they will work in the West. They help the rich, the poor and everyone in between. They know no limits as to sex, age or race. From the heart of God, through the pen of an apostle, to your conflict situation and ours, they are required tools in any strategy for conflict management.

First, we need to work out our differences <u>until we reach quality resolutions</u>.

Therefore, my beloved...work out your own salvation

The phrase *work out your own salvation* simply means to be steadfast in finding resolutions to problems. But to demonstrate this a little biblical commentary is in order concerning the term *salvation* in verse twelve. Generally, when we hear this word we immediately think of our eternal position with God. Our mental exercises lead us to the issue of whether or not we are saved. Salvation in this aspect refers to the fact that only through faith in our Lord Jesus can redemption from sin and the gift of eternal life be received. So is this what Paul had in mind when he said *work out your own salvation?*

No. Instead, Paul refered to the care and attention that

should be given toward internal problems facing the Philippian Church. But does the term *salvation* lend itself to this interpretation?

W.E. Vine, in his Expository Dictionary of New Testament Words, draws our attention to the various meanings behind this word. Included in his exposition is the following concerning one of the New Testament usages of the word *salvation*: "...the present experience of God's power to deliver from the bondage of sin, e.g., Phil. 2:12, where the special, though not the entire, reference is to the maintenance of peace and harmony."*

Vine's testimony is supported by a fundamental rule of biblical interpretation: always interpret according to the context. Both the immediate and surrounding contexts of of this passage deal with the internal unity of the body of believers in the city of Philippi, not the personal and eternal salvation of individual believers. It seems best then to understand this passage as being consistent with the apostle's flow of thought: if the Philippians plan to be a united church by developing solid relationships they will need to maintain internal peace and harmony by working together at solving problems. Put another way, their salvation experienced in Christ should have a public dimension that creates an environment of tranquillity.

So, the sense of *salvation* in this passage is defined by the

---

* Vine W.E Vine's Expository Dictionary of N.T.
Words. MacDonald Pub. Co.: McLean, Virginia; p. 998.

lack of unity in the Philippian Church and the context of verses 14-18. The issue was their bickering. He desired of them a more Christ-like attitude toward one another. This was the dilemma from which they needed to be saved.

If then there is always a need to work out our differences until we reach quality resolutions, what basis do we have for accomplishing the task? Paul helps us here also with four subordinate thoughts that qualify and clarify our first principle...**we need to work out our differences until we reach quality resolutions**.

A.   Working out our differences until we reach quality resolutions must become a matter of habit.

as you have always obeyed, not as in my presence only, but now much more in my absence

Paul preferred that the Philippians go forward with their problem solving rather than waiting for him to return. His presence was not necessary for either motivation or mediation. They should accomplish this task willingly, freely, and without hesitation. In fact, reaching quality resolutions through love and kindness, according to the apostle, should have been second nature for them.

Likewise, if we, as with the Philippian believers, need an outside stimulus to prod us toward this end then we are still in great need of work in this area. We cannot allow fear, anger, frustration, inexperience, or apathy to prevent us from turning conflict resolution skills into habits. It will not do to wait for someone else, some magical moment, or, that ever so elusive hope… "maybe it will all just go away."

B.   Working out our differences until we reach quality resolutions <u>comes through an attitude of humility</u>.

with fear and trembling

The word *fear* is typical of that emotional state wherein anxiety and tension are elevated due to some presence. The word *trembling* describes behavior associated with an emotional state characterized by *fear*. Together they graphically describe a person or group who is not terribly impressed with personal or collective abilities. The reverential awe that we should experience in the presence of God is a good illustration of this *fear and trembling*. In essence we call it humility.

When we are marked by a deep sense of humility both in the presence of God and in the presence of others we are prepared to work toward quality resolutions. When humility floods our soul we begin to think less of ourselves and more of others. This is not low self-esteem. It is not a worm-like view of ourselves. Rather, it is a high view of the value of others. *Fear and trembling* describe an attitude that sees relationships as far more important than some petty and personal hobby horse.

C.   Working out our differences until we reach quality resolutions <u>requires dependence upon God</u>.

for it is God who works in you both to will and to do

God himself desires to see his people work out their troubles. So, he has purposed to empower us toward that end. In doing so, he can create within us the will to resolve our differences and provide the way for complete success and victory.

D.   Working out our differences until we reach quality resolutions <u>creates an environment of good will</u>.

for His good pleasure

The *good pleasure* that God intends to produce for himself is that pleasure that comes as a result of seeing his people in harmony through fruitful fellowship. When we work out our differences and difficulties among ourselves on a routine basis with an attitude of humility it produces a loving environment of good-will for us and God is well pleased concerning us.

Slow down for a few moments. Think about this. One must wonder…can there be a greater motivation or better reward than knowing that God takes pleasure in us?

However, there is more. We not only need to work out our differences <u>until we come to a quality resolution</u>, we also need to do so without hurting one another. So, Paul gives us another primary principle…

Second, we need to work out our differences <u>without destroying one another</u>.

do all things without complaining and disputing

Whatever our differences may be they must be worked out through gentleness and love. Contrary to some popular notions, it will never do to allow the fervor of our emotions or convictions to step roughly upon those who disagree with us. This is what Paul had in mind when he said *do all things without complaining and disputing.*

The *all things* Paul had in mind include the very life we lead: our activities, our functions, our relationships, etc. The word *complaining* literally means to grumble and mutter. It is the act of talking negatively in hushed and secretive tones. The word *disputing* means to question and to deliberate. In our present context it involves that ugly kind of questioning and deliberation that seldom finds favor and often finds fault in others. Taken together, a clear picture of dissension and argument develops. These quarrels were not directed at those outside the family of God, but rather at others within the family of God. All this would accomplish was the destruction of one another as believers in the Church of Philippi.

There were reasons Paul wanted them to work out their differences without destroying one another. Two of these reasons are the stability of the church's public testimony and the safeguarding of biblical doctrine. So, once again, we find supporting qualifiers for our second primary principle...**we need to work out our differences <u>without destroying one another</u>.**

A.   Working out our differences without destroying one another <u>enables the church to be a positive testimony in the world.</u>

One of the by-products of a beautiful church—a church moving in harmony—is its attractiveness to the lost. When people see real love in action within the church, even in the details of our differences, they will be impressed, intrigued and interested by our testimony.

Paul provided the Philippian Church with three items that, when practiced diligently, could help establish them as a church with a positive testimony. They are not only practical, but brilliant.

1.   To remain a positive testimony in the world <u>our behavior must be above reproach</u>.

that you may become blameless and harmless,
children of God without fault

Blameless means living so as not to receive any negative criticism. *Harmless* means pure and without worldly contaminates. Paul desired of the Philippians that they trade in their ungodly attitude and behavior, characterized by their *complaining and disputing*, for the godly attitude and behavior associated with being above reproach. Rather than strife, turmoil and backbiting, they needed peace, selflessness and kindness. So do we.

The phrase *children of God without fault* is indicative of the new family roots from which Christians stem. The lineage of the Philippian Church (as well as every Christ-centered church) is no longer from the Family of Man, but from the Family of God. The former can afford family breakdowns, the latter cannot. This is the high calling to which every believer is summoned. Think of it the next time conflict is in need of resolution.

   2.   To remain a positive testimony in the world <u>we must not separate from the world.</u>

in the midst of a crooked and perverse generation, among whom you shine as lights in the world

The sphere of operation for believers—in Philippi and every place and time—is in the midst of a *crooked and perverse generation.* We can't *shine as lights in the world* if we withdraw from the world. Saints must be resolved to walk the streets of darkness, not simply walk within the halls of our churches. Holy huddles are fine for prayer, study, encouragement, and accountibilty, but failing to share truth in the world, well...that's failure.

   3.   To remain a positive testimony in the world <u>we must hold to the truth of the gospel</u>.

holding fast the word of life

The phrase *the word of life* is another way of saying the truth of the Gospel. Only in so far as the Philippian Christians would grasp the eternal fact of Jesus Christ crucified, dead, buried, resurrected and ascended, and its related life-liberating truths, would they truly remain witnesses. From this comes solid testimony. From this comes the opportunity to make a difference. Without a commitment to the historical gospel of Jesus Christ we might just as well quit!

B.　　　Working out our differences without destroying one another <u>enables us to uphold the apostolic witness</u>.

so that I may rejoice in the day of Christ that I have not run in vain or labored in vain. Yes, and if I am being poured out as a drink offering on the sacrifice and service of your faith, I am glad and rejoice with you all. For the same reason you also be glad and rejoice with me.

The Apostle Paul was dedicated. He was faithful in the proclamation of the good-news concerning Jesus Christ. Never would he tolerate another gospel. Never would he slouch in its presentation. Would the Church of Philippi uphold this great and awesome undertaking? Would they stand firm with Paul in the preservation of God's life saving good-news? If they would, then they had to refrain from destroying one another with their bickering, their fighting, and their gossiping.

It is no different for us.

Notice Paul's emphasis here: he looked forward to a time—*the day of Christ*—in which he would be filled with joy on account of the perseverance of the Philippian believers. Through godly internal harmony they could prove that his work among them was for real. They could demonstrate that the message of the gospel had indeed been accepted. They could be confident that Jesus Christ was indeed their Lord and Savior.

The same is true for believers of any city, any time.

45

When believers act the way the Lord has asked believers to act we demonstrate the reliability of our Lord's work for us and within us. In doing so we uphold the validity of the historical and apostolic truth of the gospel. When believers react toward one another with strife, animosity, and quarreling we are in effect tearing down the gospel. We are as much as saying, "What we talk, we will not walk, because really we do not believe it."

Paul knew this. He was a realist. He knew what could easily befall him in the not too distant future—death. It was his hope that if he was to be *poured out as a drink offering* it would be for a good cause. He wanted his gospel work among the Philippians to have been effective. The worst thing he could think of was that maybe he had *run in vain or labored in vain*. These were words and thoughts of great motivation. It was the diplomatic way of saying, "Listen, you Philippian believers, did you or did you not believe in and accept Jesus Christ as your Savior when I told you about Him? If you did, then please, please act toward one another accordingly…like Jesus asks of you."

What about us?

Application

Reading Step

Read through Philippians. Now read through Philippians 2 several more times. Read with intention. Read for retention. Read with devotion.

Thinking Step

Of course, movement in the direction of this chapter will directly depend on whether or not we live up to everything Paul wrote. The question then is who or what deserves priority: self or Jesus and others? If it's the former, pray and get real busy. If it's the latter, praise God and stay busy. In both cases, review and practice these foundational principles until they become almost second nature.

Theme: If we desire to build solid relationships we need to understand some principles for working out our differences.

First, we need to work out our differences <u>until we reach quality resolutions</u>.

A.   Working out our differences until we reach quality resolutions <u>must become a matter of habit</u>.

B.   Working out our differences until we reach quality resolutions <u>comes through an attitude of humility</u>.

C.   Working out our differences until we reach quality resolutions <u>requires dependence upon God</u>.

D.   Working out our differences until we reach quality resolutions <u>creates an environment of good will</u>.

Second: We need to work out our differences <u>without destroying one another</u>.

A.   Working out our differences without destroying one another <u>enables the church to be a positive testimony in the world.</u>

    1.   To remain a positive testimony in the world <u>our behavior must be above reproach</u>.

    2.   To remain a positive testimony in the world <u>we must not separate from the world.</u>

    3.   To remain a positive testimony in the world <u>we must hold to the truth of the gospel</u>.

B.   Working out our differences without destroying one another <u>enables us to uphold the apostolic witness</u>.

Moving Out Step

Take a mental stock of any differences standing between you and those you love. This may require some good ol' fashioned pondering, but go ahead. Take about thirty minutes of quiet time, pray, jog your memory, mull the whole issue over.

If you find there are indeed some differences standing between you and someone else consider whether the gulf between the two of you is in fact worth it? Now keep in mind we're not referring to basic Christian doctrines that separate believers from unbelievers, but to those opinions, emotions, methods and preferences that so often divide marriages, families, friendships, teams, businesses, and churches.

So how do we begin to bridge the gulf? Look back at the above outline. These principles are the least we can do if reaching quality resolutions is our true desire. You will need to make sure your priorities match those from Philippians 2:12-18. In a few moments, you might want to complete an exercise that may help you determine how well you match up to these principles.

But first consider the following questions:

Do your differences exist on account of your own unfulfilled expectations?

Do your differences exist due to variant philosophies?

Do your differences exist due to laziness or cowardice on your part (i.e. are you unwilling to work toward a resolution)?

Do your differences exist due to a struggle over control (i.e. who is going to have the final say)?

Answering questions like these can often expose the lingering self-centered habits of who we were before coming to the Savior. If we find that our own egos continue to cause conflict we need to check in with God. Time alone with him for some serious soul searching is probably in order.

Finally, utilize the exercise on the following pages to determine where you stand with regards to these principles for conflict resolution. You may discover some strengths and weaknesses that have gone undetected. Improving on your strengths and overcoming your weaknesses can take some time. It can also be a continual act of worship.

Principles for Conflict Resolution: A Personal Evaluation

On a scale of 1 to 5—1 being poor, 5 being good—make a good faith effort at evaluating yourself on these conflict resolution principles.

Do you typically work out differences *until you reach a quality resolution*? 1 2 3 4 5

Are you committed to reaching quality resolutions *as a matter of habit*? 1 2 3 4 5

Are you usually characterized by a *humble attitude* as you work toward quality resolutions? 1 2 3 4 5

Are you *dependent upon God* through prayer as you work toward quality resolutions? 1 2 3 4 5

Do you typically work out differences *without causing others any harm*? 1 2 3 4 5

Are you recognized as someone who *maintains a solid testimony* of Christian faith during conflict resolution?
  1 2 3 4 5

Are you recognized as someone with *impeccable integrity* in the midst of conflict?   1 2 3 4 5

Are you recognized as someone who *does not retreat from society* in the midst of conflict?   1 2 3 4 5

Are you recognized as someone with a *firm grip on the truth of the gospel* and its implications for life?
                                        1 2 3 4 5

Now to the difficult task. Ask someone else to make the same evaluation of you.

Find someone. Photocopy the following pages and give it a go.

After you receive the evaluation back, compare it to your own evaluation. Consider the contrasts. Pray about any weak areas. Thank God for your strengths.

Principles for Conflict Resolution:
An Interpersonal Evaluation

On a scale of 1 to 5—1 being poor, 5 being good—please make a current, sincere, and realistic, attempt to evaluate _____ with the following questions. (This is not a scientific tool. It is simply an interpersonal tool used only for the benefit of personal growth.)

Does _____ ...

typically work out differences until he/she reaches a quality resolution?   1 2 3 4 5

Is _____ ...

committed to reaching quality resolutions as a matter of habit?   1 2 3 4 5

usually characterized by a humble attitude while working toward quality resolutions?   1 2 3 4 5

dependent upon God through prayer while working toward quality resolutions?   1 2 3 4 5

Does _____ ...

typically work out differences without causing others any harm?   1 2 3 4 5

Is _____ ...

recognized as someone who maintains a solid testimony
of Christian faith during conflict resolution?

                                            1 2 3 4 5

recognized as someone with impeccable integrity even in
the midst of conflict?   1 2 3 4 5

recognized as someone who does not retreat from society
in the midst of conflict?   1 2 3 4 5

recognized as someone with a firm grip on the truth of
the gospel and its implications for life?   1 2 3 4 5

Thank you very much. Please return this evaluation as
soon as possible.

Much of this chapter has been adapted from portions of this author's unpublished Commentary on the New Testament Letter to the Philippians.

Attitudes for Conflict Resolution

Based Upon the Bible's Definitive Description of Love: 1 Corinthians 13

Many counselors rightly surmise that communication difficulties will almost always create problems in a relationship. When we cannot talk to one another on the same wave-length we cannot understand one another. When understanding slips from our grasp we have no basis for negotiation. Eventually we break off every attempt to communicate. Then the silence comes. Once silence gets the upper hand...

Well, you know the rest.

Likewise, if we observe the human condition long enough, we will find an even more basic problem. We call it by many names. It's our mindset. It's our internal choice producer. We call it the heart of man. Simply put, it's attitude.

Together communication and attitude have potential... either for good or for evil. Here's what it looks like...

It was attitude that took out yet another marriage. They were in their twenties. They were the parents of two beautiful children. What had started so well was unraveling quickly. He developed a miserable, chronic, and hurtful problem. She endured it, but she suffered the sting of internal wounds. The problem was alcoholism. It left its smell on every facet of their young lives and in every corner of their family.

Their time together became a proving ground for her coping skills. He could not or would not share the load of raising the children or caring for the home. Extended family relationships—what there was left of them—strained under her lonely efforts. Bills mounted. Floor space deteriorated. Access to God through prayer alone stood between her and a breakdown.

Then what he thought was impossible happened. Late one night, overcome with heartache, he gave his broken heart to Christ. The old man dropped dead. The new man came alive. His life changed that night.

Within a few days the fog lifted. Once again, he could see clearly. Every new morning erased more of his fuzzy thinking. Each new night he went to bed with vivid memories and high hopes.

Soon he began to assume responsibility. She was elated. The first six months rushed by like a wind of bliss. It was a second honeymoon.

However...

However, for every inch of responsibility he reassumed, she lost an inch of control. Now that he could think again, he began to inquire about debt. He eagerly paid attention to the children's school work. He even attended parent-teacher meetings. Making up for lost time, he called the doctor to schedule appointments. He invited in-laws over for weekend cook-outs. He planned their first vacation. He began to manage the checking account.

At first she was delighted. Later she discovered a new problem. While he lived in a state of alcoholic stupor, she lit the fires. She made everything go round. Now she was a partner. Now she needed negotiation skills. This new stage of life pulled her between ecstasy and exasperation. Soon the exasperation dominated the tug-of-war.

She found herself quarreling over issues she once longed to have lifted from her shoulders. He was surprised. She was frustrated. Their honeymoon joy lost ground to interpersonal conflict.

She once thought the removal of alcohol would end their nightmares. He once thought the same thing. She once thought his willingness to help out would create the perfect marriage. He once thought his new found willingness to lead would set his wife upon a pedestal. They were wrong. The removal of alcohol, while a true blessing, paved the way for a new round of learning. All the old skills—her in charge, him in a stupor—were overturned. Their marriage needed serious renegotiation.

With the tables now turned, he sought counsel (like she used to do) and she withdrew into a shell (like he used to do). He began to grow. She began to shrink. Friends, family, and their pastor tried to help, but the years had taken their toll. She felt broken. He was dismayed. From her brokenness grew an attitude of defeat. From his dismay grew an attitude of indifference. And from broken and misguided attitudes there grew broken and misguided communication. Soon they just quit talking to one another. They drifted apart. It was not explosive. Just sad. Sad and needless and wrong.

You see, the relationship between communication and attitude is too close to dissect. Our Lord Jesus once said, *But the things that come out of the mouth come from the heart, and these make a man 'unclean.' For out of the heart come evil thoughts, murder, adultery, sexual immorality, theft, false testimony, slander.* (Matthew 15:18,19 NIV). No wonder so many books, seminars, classes and college courses designed to increase communication fail to produce. When we fail to address the core issue of poor communication—attitude—no amount of technique will overcome the problem.

So, what then is the answer for attitudes in need of adjustment? And, if we find the answer will it help the process of communication as we attempt to resolve relational conflicts? The answer to the first question is love. The second answer is yes. Notice what the Apostle Paul said to the troubled Church of Corinth: *If I had the gift of being able to speak in other languages without learning them, and could speak in every language there is in all of heaven and earth, but didn't love others, I would only be making noise* (1 Corinthians 13:1 Living Bible). In more traditional translations of this verse the phrase "making noise" is rendered "clanging cymbal or noisy gong." The meaning can't be missed. No matter how gifted an individual is a lack of love nullifies his abilities.

Why? The answer is not all that difficult. The human condition will not allow for a prolonged attitude vacuum. Something must fill the emptiness within. If not love, then anger, resentment, bitterness, indifference and/or the like. And, as Jesus said, *whatever is on the inside will make itself known on the outside.*

When the Apostle Paul addressed the Corinthian Church regarding this issue of love he did so while speaking about certain problems in the church. The particular problem he had in mind was the misuse of spiritual gifts. In chapter 12, Paul pointed out that there are many gifts, but one Giver; many church members, but one Church. As the gifts and the church members are brought together the Giver—God the Holy Spirit—expects everyone to benefit. In other words, spiritual gifts are intended for the edification of the whole, not the individual member receiving a particular gift.

In chapter 14, Paul took up the specific problem of how the Corinthian Church was abusing one particular spiritual gift—the gift of languages. By contrasting the gift of languages with the gift of prophecy, Paul alerted his readers to one very important fact—the same fact described in chapter 12: spiritual gifts are designed to build up the whole. When they edify one at the expense of others they are being misused. Prophecy is always other-centered. The abuse of the gift of languages—as used in Corinth—remained self-centered.

What does all this have to do with The Love Chapter: 1 Corinthians 13? Everything. You see, chapter 13 comes smack dab in the middle of this theological discourse on the spiritual gifts. It is an illustration of the Apostle Paul's point concerning other-centeredness. If we want to know which direction the spiritual gifts should flow we need only look upon love. Love, in its purest form, looks out for the well-being of others. Love denies self and upholds others. Paul wanted his readers to understand that the gifts were designed the same way. They were meant to build up others for the benefit of the whole. What better illustration could he find beyond love?

Love is the core attitude upon which every successful relationship exists. It is also the core attitude through which all conflict resolution occurs. It is the foundation from which we receive the needed motivation to resolve conflict. Without love we will go our separate ways. If even slowly, our relationship will start to fade.

1 Corinthians 13:4-7 contains fifteen qualities of love. When they are present in our lives, it is a safe bet our attitudes toward others will be helpful not harmful. And this is what we're looking for—attitudes that make things better not bitter. Right? So, once again, open your Bible. Turn to 1 Corinthians 13, pray, ask the Lord for guidance, and let's start looking at a few of these characteristics of love up close and personal.

Let's get focused by boiling our passage down to a simple theme statement:

If we desire to build solid relationships we must <u>have loving attitudes while working out our differences</u>.

Love is patient, love is kind. It does not envy, it does not boast, it is not proud. It is not rude, it is not self-seeking, it is not easily angered, it keeps no record of wrongs. Love does not delight in evil but rejoices with the truth. It always protects, always trusts, always hopes, always perseveres. 1 Corinthians 13:4-7 (NIV)

In this little segment of Scripture, we learn more about love than philosophers and poets have been able to provide for centuries. We learn that love is more than good vibrations. This kind of love does something. It changes our behaviors. It compels us to be the best we can be for others. It causes us to become more like Jesus. What better example can we think of as motivation for conflict resolution as we seek to build and maintain the very best relationships possible.

Now consider eight (two are combined under number seven) of love's qualities that apply to attitudes necessary for conflict resolution. (There are seven more, but we'll leave those for the application at the end of the chapter.)

First, possessing a loving attitude while working out differences <u>means we must avoid interruptions and instead be patient.</u>

Love is patient...

Love being *patient* simply means hanging in there with another person. It means that when we love we should not be too hasty with another. Should we apply this to our communication skills we will benefit greatly. Why? In simple terms it comes down to this: when we interrupt we demonstrate a greater appreciation for our own thoughts than for our partner in communication. They will very quickly realize this. Soon thereafter they will do the same. It should not happen, because if love means anything it means getting past self for the well-being of those we care about.

Second, possessing a loving attitude while working out differences <u>means we must avoid retaliation and instead be kind</u>.

Love...is kind

The second characteristic of love found in 1 Corinthians 13:4 is kindness. The meaning rests with simplicity, but explodes with power. There is no mystery in what it means to be kind. However, keep this in mind: from God's point of view, biblical love extends kindness even to those who offer abuse.

Consider how far such an attitude can go in the process of conflict resolution. The Book of Proverbs tells us that *a gentle answer turns away wrath, but a harsh word stirs up anger* (Proverbs 15:1 NIV). The reliability of this maxim is verified through the experience of every man, woman, and child. When we retaliate against an aggressor he or she never thinks warm-fuzzies about us. Instead, the aggressor finds provocation for further anger. The aggressor may feel whipped or the aggressor may turn and start doing some verbal whipping, but in either case the aggressor's attitudes are burning, not soothing.

However, kindness has a way of winning the day while retaliation only seems to escalate hostilities. When we serve our aggressor, we provide him or her with an opportunity to cool off, to slow down, and to refocus his or her emotion. It may be true that kindness will not always be met with a similar response. Sometimes our kindness is taken for granted. Sometimes it's ignored. Sometimes it's even abused. Yet, we must persevere for several reasons.

The first reason is easy...kindness is right. The second reason is practical. So, okay, everyone knows kindness is sometimes met with hostility. Maybe our good faith efforts at kindness do not produce the desired effect. Still, its success rate will be far better than fighting fire with fire. While kindness may not always bring about a similar response from another, retaliation will never bring about peace, tranquillity or harmony—at best it will only subdue an opponent. And, we must always remember, an opponent subdued is an enemy in waiting. The third reason is personal. It stems from some basic questions: "What kind of people do we want to be? In the final analysis do we want to hang our heads in shame over our lack of love or do we want to know we have done all that we could through loving kindness to resolve conflict?" The answer seems almost too easy.

Third, possessing a loving attitude while working out differences <u>means we must avoid over-assertiveness and instead be humble</u>.

Love...it is not proud

The last phrase in 1 Corinthians 13:4 tells us that love *is not proud*. The New King James Bible translates this as *Love...is not puffed up*. The New American Standard Version renders the same phrase as *Love...is not arrogant*. The meaning is this: other-centered and sacrificial love is not self-assertive.

So, what are we to make of this? The world would think us crazy for accepting the notion that assertiveness is wrong. However, Christlike communication travels on heavenly, not earthly wisdom. Consider the effect Jesus had upon our world by choosing the humble way over the assertive way. Listen to the words of Peter: *To this you were called, because Christ suffered for you, leaving you an example, that you should follow in his steps. 'He committed no sin, and no deceit was found in his mouth.' When they hurled their insults at him, he did not retaliate; when he suffered, he made no threats. Instead, he entrusted himself to him who judges justly. He himself bore our sins in his body on the tree, so that we might die to sins and live for righteousness; by his wounds you have been healed* (1 Peter 2:21-24 NIV).

Does this mean we should accept physical abuse and the like? No! We're not dealing with those extremes right now. Rather the issue addressed here is whether or not we are willing to give up our wants, desires, and needs. The question each of us must face is this: "Must I always win the argument?" It has everything to do with attitude.

Self-assertiveness training may not actually go so far as to advocate winning at the expense of another every time, but it would insist upon advocating for our personal agenda in the midst of every conflict. This presumably will create the best outcome. Why? Self-assertiveness training would say we cannot help others until we are satisfied with ourselves. For the so-called wisdom of our age this is a hallmark of true maturity and love. Yet, a rose by any other name is still fragrant and skunk cabbage by any other name is still foul. Our attitude is either humble or it is not.

We may rationalize our self-assertion by saying, "Well, if I don't get my point across, who will do it for me? And if I don't make my point then who knows what might happen." Still, all things being equal, this is not just self-protection. It is the reality of pride. It is the evidence for Ecclesiastes 7:20 (NIV): *There is not a righteous man on earth who does what is right and never sins.*

Fourth, possessing a loving attitude while working out differences <u>means we must avoid selfishness and instead be other-centered</u>.

Love...is not self-seeking

In verse five we find that love is *not self-seeking*. It means we are not to be self-centered. This is similar to, but not exactly the same as not being over-assertive. While over-assertiveness tends to create problems for communication while we are in a conflict episode, self-centeredness creates problems over the long term. One is pushy at times, the other is pushy all the time. For love to not be self-seeking it must never be pushy.

In the area of communication this is vital. True listening is not simply the silence of our own lips. Instead, we should be very attentive to the other person. If we are spending time formulating what we're going to say next we are not really listening to others. As a result, communication does not really take place. This, in just plain English, is selfishness. The antidote for selfishness is the mind of Jesus Christ. His eternal pattern always has been, still is, and always shall be other-centered (Philippians 2:5-11).

Communication experts tell us that one way to overcome selfish communication patterns is to develop a win-win attitude as opposed to a win-lose attitude. In the win-lose frame of mind we concentrate on how we can defeat the other person with our reasons, our evidence, our logic or even the quantity of our words. With a win-win attitude our thoughts are concerned with what is best for everyone. When we live with this in mind we have a greater capacity for accepting the ideas of others. When we're willing and desirous to consider the ideas of another we are better prepared to listen as they speak.

Fifth, possessing a loving attitude while working out differences <u>means we must avoid resentment and instead be forgiving</u>.

Love...keeps no record of wrongs

Love...keeps no record of wrongs! Wow! When tomorrow comes yesterday's pains should be considered historical, not contemporary. However, we too often continue to resurface yesterday's wrongs. Instead of an attitude of forgiveness we harbor attitudes of resentment.

We say things like: "Oh yeah, well just don't forget about how you broke your promise on our last anniversary!" Or, "Your always overdrawing the checking account. Won't you ever learn?" There may be much truth in statements like these, but they are still ineffective patterns for communication.

Why? Well, they betray our unwillingness to forbear. Instead, statements like these reveal our tendency for harboring a grudge, for keeping a tally ledger of wrongs done to us. It's called resentment. It's the opposite of forgiveness. It's an attitude altogether contrary to love. It is precisely what the Apostle Paul wanted us to avoid.

And why is this such a big deal? Why should we leave the past in the past? Here's why...

While forgiveness is a hallmark of love, resentment is a hallmark of bitterness, anger and, eventually, hate. The final outcome of attitudes like these is not difficult to forecast. Left uncorrected, attitudes like these produce death...the death of love. When love dies friendships die, marriages die, churches die, families die. Conflict is never resolved. It is only swept under the rug.

Now think for a moment how absurd it would be to literally sweep dust under your rug over and over and over again. After the first few days of this process there would still not be much of an observable impact on the rug. Let a few months of this process go by and you will have a considerable problem.

Right in the middle of your rug will arise a lump. You, your family, your relatives, and your friends now have to sit in the room, see the lump, but say absolutely nothing about it. You will attempt conversations. You will hope to carry on as though nothing were wrong. Yet all of you will be painfully aware of the lump. You can attempt to dance around it or try to ignore it. You may trip over it and try to shrug it off, but you won't.

Ridiculous, right? Of course it is when we are only talking about dust. However, every day, all over the world people play this silly game with one another. We think, "Maybe, if I just ignore it, it will go away." But it does not. The resentment is still there. Like any ugly lump, sooner or later, it will be in the way. We <u>will</u> trip over it. If it is not replaced with forgiveness, resentment will mess up our living space.

Sixth, possessing a loving attitude while working out differences <u>means we must avoid presumption and instead be trusting</u>.

Love...always trusts

Verse seven includes a small phrase teaching us that love *always trusts*. The New King James Version of the Bible translates that phrase as love *believes all things*. The Contemporary English Version translates the phrase simply as *loyal*. To trust, to believe all things, to be loyal does not require that we become gullible. It means we are willing to give others the benefit of the doubt. It means we will believe the best about people. We cannot presume to know what another is thinking or feeling. To do so leads us into the trap of jumping to unwarranted and undesirable conclusions.

The answer to this problem is patient and active listening. When the opportunity arises we should restate what we think the other person has just said. This gives our communication partner a chance to indicate whether or not we have correctly understood what he or she has said. For example, suppose a wife should say to her husband, "I'm really tired, I've just got to get some sleep." The husband can read this in any of several ways. He could think his wife is disinterested in him sexually. He could think she has been busy with too many interests outside the context of their marriage and family. He could think she is becoming ill. Or, among other things, he could simply accept her statement at face value. His attitude will make the difference.

Should he choose to avoid presumption he may very well come out ahead. Should he jump to an unwarranted conclusion, he might respond something like this: "You're always too tired. My needs mean nothing to you!!" Through presumption, and, more than likely, some apparent frustration, he just fired the opening salvo in what is sure to become a verbal fire-fight. His outburst would sure enough create some conflict, not resolve his frustration. This does not win, it loses. It loses, because it fails to trust. It loses, because it is not loving.

This presumption on his part is fuel ready for ignition. A better response would have been: "Honey, are you saying you've had too much to do lately. Sometimes I feel like we have so very little time together. Is there anything else you would like me to understand? Is there anything I can do to lighten your load?" This active listening and gentle probing may allow his wife to recommunicate the simple intentions of her statement. If there *is* something deeper, it may allow her the safety and freedom to express other concerns or thoughts.

Seventh, possessing a loving attitude while working out differences means we must avoid quitting and instead keep trying.

Love...always hopes, always perseveres

Giving up communicates the beginning of the end for love. It means love is fading. Despair has won. Hope has lost. Perseverance has disappeared. Any further attempts at securing peace and harmony begin to be viewed as suspect. For this reason the Holy Spirit inspired the Apostle Paul to finish verse seven of 1 Corinthians 13 with (love) *always hopes, always perseveres.*

Hope and perseverance continue to look forward. Hope always provides a second chance. Hope yearns for something far better. Perseverance remains steadfast. Perseverance maintains loyalty. Hope does not find a finish line in the relationship race. Perseverance endures every hardship. The two march on and on. They keep right on trying.

It would be helpful to see these qualities of love manifested in the covenant of God. Consider that God never signed a contract with mankind. Rather, he sealed a covenant with us—and covenants are not broken. (At least God will not break one.) He promised to provide new life where sin produced death. As a result of his love and mercy and grace this promise is fulfilled. The death of Jesus Christ upon the cross covered our responsibility to pay for sin. The debt we owe, he paid. When we accept this free gift through Jesus Christ we accept God's gracious provision of eternal life.

Yet, if we look back upon the history of mankind, we can see God would have been justified at any point along the line to give up on us. Still, he did not and he has not. He constantly provides that second chance. We sin. He forgives. We run. He pursues. We hide. He seeks. We rebel. He loves. We stubbornly refuse his offers of reconciliation. He patiently awaits our offer of contrition.

Hope is like that...it keeps on keeping on. Perseverance is like that...it sticks to it. Were these applied in relationships today we would see far less racism, far less ageism, far less sexism, far less elitism. Were these applied in relationships today we would see far fewer divorces, far fewer broken families, far fewer split churches, far fewer failed businesses. Perseverance and hope are far too hidden in many lives. How about yours?

As we begin to wrap up this chapter on attitude, consider what Henry Drummond in The Greatest Thing In The World wrote: "No form of vice, not worldliness, nor greed of gold, nor drunkenness itself, does more to unChristianize society than evil temper. For embittering life, for breaking up communities, for destroying the most sacred relationships; for devastating homes, for withering up men and women, for taking the bloom off childhood; in short, for sheer gratuitous misery-producing power, this influence—an angry temper—stands alone." He was absolutely right.

He was right because an angry temper is the product of a selfish attitude. It's an attitude that says, "Me first!" No amount of rationalizing will change this fact. Blame it on others. Call it something else. Ignore its presence. Do what we will. Still, anger out of control stems from an attitude of selfishness. And the only answer is love. Love that sacrifices the whims of self-preoccupation for the well-being of others. Now that's proper attitude. Conflict resolution requires it.

If we only know the technical side—the principles and methods—yet fail to appropriate right attitudes we are in trouble. Many people know what they should do, but do not want to do it. Remember the Apostle Paul's words: *If I speak in the tongues of men and of angels, but have not love, I am only a resounding gong or a clanging cymbal* (1 Corinthians 13:1). No matter how able or how gifted we are, efforts without love blow away in the wind.

Attitudes. Love. Conflict Resolution. They go together.

Application

Reading Step

Read through 1 Corinthians 13 again. Now read it several more times. Did you notice those qualities of love in verses 4-7 that we did not comment upon?

Vs. 4 *Love...does not envy, it does not boast.*

Love *does not envy* means that love is not displeased with another's success. Likewise, *it does not boast* means love does not allow us to focus upon our own merits.

Vs. 5 *Love...is not rude...it is not easily angered.*

Amplified, these phrases mean that love prevents us from acting disgracefully or indecently and love keeps us from being irritable, touchy, or easily offended.

Vs. 6 *Love does not delight in evil but rejoices with the truth.*

This sentence means that love finds absolutely no joy in evil, wickedness, or unrighteousness. Instead, love finds joy in truth and honesty.

Vs. 7 *Love...always protects.*

Finally, this phrase means love causes us to cover the things that displease us. Love keeps us from exposing the deficiencies of others. Love bears all things.

Thinking Step

When you think of love, as described in 1 Corinthians 13, who comes to mind? Could it be someone close to you? Maybe Mom or Dad? Husband or wife? Brother or sister? Maybe your friend? A former teacher?

If thinking about love helps you recall this special person, why? Is it because you see in this person some of these qualities? Probably so. Would you like to be considered as that special someone in yet another person's life? Moreover, what if thinking about love does not bring to your mind someone special? What if you only feel pain and hurt instead of love when you think of others? What then? Who will be your role model? How will you believe in love if you have not experienced it very well from those in your life?

Listen please to the greatest book on conflict resolution ever written:

For God so loved the world that he gave his one and only Son, that whoever believes in him shall not perish but have eternal life (John 3:16 NIV).

But God demonstrates his own love for us in this: While we were still sinners, Christ died for us (Romans 5:8 NIV).

This is how God showed his love among us: He sent his one and only Son into the world that we might live through him. This is love: not that we loved God, but that he loved us and sent his Son as an atoning sacrifice for our sins (1 John 4:9,10 NIV).

If you are hurting from the absence of real love turn your heart toward God. He longs to fill your heart with his infinite love. Accept the provision of his grace, his mercy, his peace...his love. Talk with him. Cry out. Ask him...Lord Jesus, Father in heaven, be my all in all.

Let him resolve the greatest conflict in your life—the alienation you experience from him. As he reconciles you toward himself, he will begin to help you find the strength, the knowledge, and the capacity to reconcile with others as well.

Moving Out Step

How often have you really taken time to think through these fifteen qualities of love? Do you ever take time to evaluate your ownership of these qualities? Do you own all of them? Any of them? None of them?

What areas need your immediate attention? What areas are you strong in? How can you develop the former and improve the latter? Perhaps the exercise beginning on the next page can help.

Note: Be careful of who you select for this exercise. You must be well enough informed to be accurately confident (not assumed confidence) he or she will not use your invitation to download his or her agenda, baggage, or immaturity...leaving you worse than when you started.

Fifteen Qualities of Love: Interpersonal Evaluation

1.   This will require the assistance of another person. Choose someone you value highly and trust completely. Ask him or her to meet with you to discuss the fifteen qualities of love found in 1 Corinthains 13. Ask for input on how well you rate on each of the characteristics.

2.   Utilize the following discussion guide to facilitate your conversation. You should also have a pencil and notebook available to write down some notes as you talk.

3.   After discussing several of the characteristics, if you or your conversation partner need to take a break or need to table the discussion until another time, by all means do so. This should be enjoyable and productive. Do not allow it to become anything less.

Begin with something like this…

"Let's work our way through the fifteen qualities of love found in 1 Corinthians 13. After briefly considering the meaning of each quality, I'd like to hear your honest evaluation of how well I do regarding that characteristic. And, if you don't mind, I'd like to ask some questions along the way for the purpose of clarification. Okay?"

Be sure to let your conversation partner respond. Answer any questions to the best of your ability. Remain far, far away from any defensiveness. Remember, you are the one looking for personal growth so assure the other person you desire honest and straigthforward input.

1.   Love is patient. In fact, it is so very patient it even endures others when they are acting unlovely.

With five being high and one being low, how would you rate me on this characteristic? 1   2   3   4   5

Can you tell me why you chose that rating?

Anything else that may help me understand better?

How can I improve?

2.   Love is kind. It reacts with goodness regardless of the attitudes and actions of others.

Again, how do you see me on this one? 1   2   3   4   5

If I could make one change to improve that rating, what change would you like to see?

3.   Love does not envy. Love is not jealous over the success of another person.

Again: 1   2   3   4   5

If low, ask: What do I do or say that demonstrates envy and jealousy?

If medium or high, ask: Okay, thank you for that, but how might I do better?

4.   Love does not boast. Love is not preoccupied with self. It does not focus attention on self.

Again: 1   2   3   4   5

What difficulties do you see in my life when I'm doing poorly with this characteristic?

Anything else?

5.   Love is not proud. It is not overly assertive.

Again: 1   2   3   4   5

If little or no need for improvement, ask: Why?

If improvement is needed, ask: What could I do better?

6.   Love is not rude. It does not act crude, unseemly, improperly, coarse, or without manners.

Again: 1   2   3   4   5

Ask: Any help here or should we move along?

7.   Love is not self seeking. It is not preoccupied with self. It does not insist on having its way all the time.

Again: 1   2   3   4   5

Any positive examples of how I avoid this problem?

What does it look like when I am self seeking?

Now you're in the groove. Continue with questions of your own. If you choose to utilize a yes or no question, be sure to follow it up with an open ended question to allow the other person to explain why, what, when, etc.

8.   Love is not easily angered. It is not irritable. It is not easily offended.

Again: 1 2 3 4 5

Questions:

9.   Love keeps no record of wrongs. It does not hold on to resentment.

Again: 1 2 3 4 5

Questions:

10.   Love does not delight in evil or wrong doing.

Again: 1 2 3 4 5

Questions:

11.   Love rejoices with the truth. It is honest. It does not like deceit, cover-ups, half-truths, or innuendo.

Again: 1 2 3 4 5

Questions:

12.   Love always protects. It does does not go around exposing the deficiencies of others.

Again: 1 2 3 4 5

Questions:

13.   Love always trusts. It gives others the benefit of the doubt. It is not presumptuous.

Again: 1 2 3 4 5

Questions:

14.   Love always hopes. It does not despair. It likes to provide multiple chances.

Again: 1 2 3 4 5

Questions:

15.   Love always perseveres. It endures. It remains loyal and steadfast.

Again: 1   2   3   4   5

Questions:

Conclusion:

1.   Upon completion, thank the other person. Also, ask him or her to feel free to offer any further input at a later time should something come to mind.

2.   Keep your notes. Later go back over them. Pray about the areas you are concerned about.

3.   Find some creative and practical ways to work on those areas of concern. Have fun.

A Method for Conflict Resolution

When We Are Responsible for Conflict
Matthew 5:21-26

"That's easy for you to say, you've never been through what I'm dealing with!"

"Yes, I think you're right. Certainly, I do not know just how you feel. In fact, no one has ever experienced the exact same thing you are going through. No one ever will. No one, of course, other than Jesus. He knows exactly how you feel."

"So, how can you sit there and tell me to apologize?"

"Because it's the right thing to do. Independent of your feelings and independent of your circumstances, it's the right thing to do. In this case, the past does not matter. This time around it was you that seriously messed up. She did not deserve the verbal assault you unleashed."

"Yeah, but..."

Yeah, but... How many times had the pastor heard that before?

It was late. The pastor's eyes itched from too many hours. His head felt that nagging, dull ache prophesying a full-blown migraine. How much longer would the other man drone on about how justified his actions toward his wife had been? How many more "yeah buts" could he endure? How many more passages of Scripture would it take to convince him that yelling at his wife was wrong, just plain wrong?

"Pastor, I can't. I won't. I'm finished. I'm not going to put up with her anymore?"

"You're not going to put up with her!!!? Who do you think you are," the pastor yelled. "Haven't you heard anything I've said!!!?"

Silence. Like a dagger, sin stabbed the pastor's heart. What had he done? How could he have lost his temper? What would he say? What should he say? Silence. More silence.

"Perhaps I should leave now," the other man said.

"Yes, perhaps you should," the pastor answered.

"Goodnight."

"Goodnight. I...ah...I...um."

"It's okay pastor. I understand."

Really? Do you suppose he truly understood? Or did he just recognize that, like himself, the pastor was capable of losing his temper? Had he even come close to resolving his own problem? Had he come to grips with his own sin toward his wife? Unfortunately, probably not.

Whether we want to admit it or not, there are times when the responsibility for a breach in a relationship lies with us. Sure, there are other times when another person is responsible for the separation in a relationship. Still, at other times responsibility for the differences cannot easily be placed; or perhaps it belongs to both parties; or, in the case of a group, some or all of the parties. Regardless of which circumstance prevails, recognizing principles and attitudes necessary for conflict resolution is a great beginning. However, in some cases, we will need a step by step, line upon line methodical approach to follow should we hope for success in working out these problems and differences.

Of course, we must first determine to remain *godly* in the process of resolving conflict. Even should the fault lie with another we must remember to keep ourselves in fellowship. In Galatians 6:1 (NIV) we read, *Brothers, if someone is caught in a sin, you who are spiritual should restore him gently. But watch yourself, or you also may be tempted.* In Matthew 7:3 (NIV) we read that Jesus said, *Why do you look at the speck of sawdust in your brother's eye and pay no attention to the plank in your own eye?* We cannot stress enough the importance of self-evaluation before, during, and after any attempt at conflict resolution.

In subsequent chapters we will tackle the questions, "What do we do when another person is responsible for conflict?" and "What do we do when responsibility for conflict is difficult to place?" But before we get after those issues, let's first consider...

What do we do when we are responsible for creating problems in a relationship?

Jesus dealt with this situation while delivering the Sermon on the Mount (Matthew chapters five through seven). While illustrating the depth of righteousness necessary for a people entering the kingdom of heaven (Matthew 5:20) he used a comparison between murder and anger. It was stated in the law (Exodus 20:13), *Do not murder,* but Jesus said, *anyone who is angry with his brother will be subject to judgment* (Matthew 5:22a). Why? The answer, is this: anger towards another always divides. It always creates injury to the relationship. It is, therefore, on the other side of righteousness.

Now consider for a moment that the Lord's Sermon on the Mount has to do with *ideal* behavior and attitudes. The Sermon on the Mount describes *heavenly* character, attitude, and behavior. The intention of Matthew is to show us, through Jesus' teaching on these heavenly standards, that none of us can measure up—that is why we need a Savior. By ourselves we will always fall short. We are not perfect and we cannot earn salvation through our conduct. Yet, these ideal standards are still ideals for which we can strive (not to gain salvation, but as a demonstration of our gratitude to Christ and of our understanding that his ways are best). Therefore, with God's help, we need to pursue these truths with gusto.

So, what exactly must we pursue should we want to resolve the problem of anger lying between us and another? When the problem falls squarely upon our own shoulders, three steps come to mind based upon Matthew 5:21-26.

Here they are section by section and step by step...

Step #1: Our first step is to <u>examine our own feelings</u>.

You have heard that it was said to the people long ago, 'Do not murder, and anyone who murders will be subject to judgment.' But I tell you that anyone who is angry with his brother will be subject to judgment. Again, anyone who says to his brother, 'Raca,' is answerable to the Sanhedrin. But anyone who says, 'You fool!', will be in danger of the fire of hell. Matthew 5:21-22 (NIV)

When our emotions run out of control others get hurt. In the Hebrew culture of the first century the word *Raca* was a term of utter contempt. Used as a verbal insult it meant the other person was intellectually empty-headed. The term *fool* was even worse. It referred to a godless and moral reprobate. Words like these are spoken in haste. They erupt from emotional overload. When anger and bitterness run out of control they also run amuck with our speech. Let's face it, this is damaging to any relationship.

Yet, there are many who say the full expression of emotions is the only way to ensure one's emotional well-being? Take, for example, the following case.

The situation: Mom and Dad had divorced. Their sixth grade daughter longed to see her Daddy. When she did, he was inattentive and distant.

The problem: Unable to assist with the depression experienced after visits with Dad, Mom asked the school counselor to "talk" with her daughter. The counselor asked the little girl all the typical questions, "How do you feel," etc. After discovering her feelings, the counselor asked "What do you feel like doing about it?" The little girl was reluctant to say what she wanted to do about the problem. So the counselor encouraged her to respond.

Finally, this sad and precious child said, " I want to kick him and punch him in the stomach! I just want to tell him that I hate him. I want to call him names!"

"Like what?" the counselor asked.

"Like bleep and bleep and bleep bleep!"

"Good, that's good, get it out" the counselor said.

And so the conversation continued. In the end, the little girl was encouraged to tell her father just how she felt. She heard from this person in authority that to do less would only cause her pain to remain buried. Sooner or later the pain would eat her up.

During Daddy's next visit, she told him just what she felt. All the pain, all the frustration—in all of its vulgarity—poured out. Like acid it boiled over and burned not only dad, but the little girl and the relationship as well. Nothing was gained. Almost everything was lost. Now where would Mom look for help? She turned to the pastor of a small church. After describing the whole situation, she whispered "Can you help us? Please, I'm begging you. Can you help my little girl? Can you help me to help her? Can you?"

Slowly, the pastor opened the Bible and read, *Come to Me, all you who labor and are heavy laden, and I will give you rest. Take My yoke upon you and learn from Me, for I am gentle and lowly in heart, and you will find rest for your souls. For My yoke is easy and My burden is light."* (Matthew 11:28-30 NKJV). Then he added, "No I cannot. I cannot help you, but Jesus can. Would you like his help?"

It took time, but the little girl and her mother began to heal. They started healing because they met Christ and began to solve their problems his way. They learned that exploring their feelings should mean more than simply identifying them and acting them out. Instead of allowing their emotions to rule them, they began to rule their emotions through the power of Christ's love.

Are we saying the father of this little girl did not bear responsibility for the problems? Of course he did. It should go without saying. Yet, the responsibilities of others cannot reduce our own responsibilities.

Like this mother and her daughter, we all need to consider whether our feelings are good or evil. If they are good they may produce appropriate and mature attitudes and behaviors. If they are evil—and let there be no mistake, every man, woman and child is capable of evil emotion—they may produce destruction. Bringing our feelings under great scrutiny is the first step in dealing with conflict for which we ourselves are responsible.

We cannot escape the authority of the Lord's teaching. Jesus said the kind of emotional reaction described in Matthew 5:21,22 will bring about severe judgment. His words were clear: verbally abusing others is no better than murder. Allowing bitterness and anger to control our speech will never help. Our part, then, is to evaluate and examine our hearts in preparation for our next step.

Step #2: Our second step is to seek reconciliation.

Therefore, if you are offering your gift at the altar and there remember that your brother has something against you, leave your gift there in front of the altar. First go and be reconciled to your brother; then come and offer your gift. Matthew 5:23,24 (NIV)

Consider the context. During our Lord's time on earth, Jewish people would bring a sacrifice to the temple altar as an act of worship. They knew their sins grieved God. They knew these sins kept them from intimate fellowship with him. Therefore, they needed a way to care for the situation. God provided the altar. The sacrifice served as a payment for sin. The offering would provide the Jewish worshiper a clean slate before God. He or she would then have an open avenue of prayer.

Christians, of course, have accepted Jesus Christ. He is our ultimate sacrifice. As a result, we come directly to God in prayer. Yet, we are not free from the presence of sin. Like the Jewish person during the first century, we can sometimes be struck with the stark reality that we have caused someone offense. We sometimes remember that our *brother has something against* us. When confronted like this with our own sin, we need to stop. We need to stop and accept the simple fact that we are wrong. Before making things right with God, we need to make things right with the person we have harmed.

The point is this: if you want to be right with God then make things right with others also. Just as our personal relationship with God the Father, Son, and Holy Spirit impacts our personal relationships with others, our relationships with others impacts our relationship with God. For example, this principle is so strong that God, through the Apostle Peter, warns husbands that if they hurt their wives he will not listen to their prayers. Here is how Peter put it: *Husbands, in the same way be considerate as you live with your wives, and treat them with respect as the weaker partner and as heirs with you of the gracious gift of life, so that nothing will hinder your prayers* (1Peter 3:7 NIV).

Thus the phrase *be reconciled*, in Matthew 5:24, implies that we must work together with the other person in the process of conflict resolution. In this context our work is made simple. If another person has something against us we are responsible to make amends. Perhaps we will need to seek forgiveness on account of some offense. Maybe we will need to repay a debt owed. Whatever the problem, we must initiate healing. When the breach in a relationship begins with us we must be the one who initiates reconciliation. If and when we have gone to the other person and asked forgiveness, then, and only then, are we released to continue in worship.

Okay, that seems easy to talk about, but actually doing it...well, that is something else. In fact, perhaps the nine most difficult words in the English language are "I was wrong. I am sorry. Please forgive me."

True enough. Still, we can't escape what Jesus teaches. It may or may not result in a desired outcome. It may or may not work to our advantage. It may or may not repair the relationship. In fact, there will be times when others will choose not to forgive us. They may even grow cold or explode with anger. However, none of that matters. Christians must be motivated by principle not experience. Doing the right thing should be reward enough.

Step #3: Our third step <u>is to keep short accounts</u>.

Settle matters quickly with your adversary who is taking you to court. Do it while you are still with him on the way, or he may hand you over to the judge, and the judge may hand you over to the officer, and you may be thrown into prison. I tell you the truth, you will not get out until you have paid the last penny. Matthew 5:25,26 (NIV)

Our first step then, when we are the responsible party, is an honest self-examination. The second step is the actual act of going to the other person. Step three has to do with timing: it involves keeping short accounts. Look again at verses 25 and 26. The context here clearly has to do with a financial transaction. The principle, however, applies to many situations. Jesus would rather we take care of our problems quickly. The alternative is procrastination—which rarely helps. When reconciliation is necessary we need to move quickly before the problem grows out of control. The proverbial mountain out of a mole hill is all too real. We all know it.

Not only can we verify this sequence of events from our Lord's words, but also from our own experiences. Who has not heard of a family member, friend or acquaintance suffering from poor credit because the problem was put off and off and off? Who has not seen a relationship strained because someone refused to act on a problem quickly? Who does not know of a divorced couple who lost their direction when they quit communicating? The failure to keep short accounts usually escalates any problem. Therefore, we need to be impressed with this truth: relationships are far too important to allow the reconciliation process any delay. Short accounts are not simply smart, they are mandatory wisdom.

In old Russia, a folk-song was composed to tell the story of a procrastinating man. While he desired to have a new house, he put off building it until "everything was just right." He wanted to have just the right materials. He wanted just the right weather. He wanted a place for everything and everything in its place. Unfortunately, he died before starting construction. Here are the words of the folk-song:

And there in solemn silence stood

The piles of stone and piles of wood,
Till Death, who in his vast affairs
Ne'er puts off things as men do theirs,
Winked at our hero as he passed:
"Your house is finished, Sir, at last,
A narrow cell, a house of clay,
Your mansion for an endless day."

Coffins. Biological life forms, sooner or later, wind up in them. It need not be so with relational life. Yet, how sad it is that we so often nail shut the coffin lid over a relationship just because we put off until tomorrow what should have been reconciled today. We figure maybe the timing will be better tomorrow. We cling to the notion that time might heal all wounds. We hope mutual understanding goes without saying. We think if we let it go long enough it will just be forgotten. But these are mere wishful thoughts...dreams without substance. In actual truth, we know better. We know putting it off is sometimes just caused by stubbornness. At other times pride gets in the way. At yet other times it might be fear or perhaps laziness or even ignorance. What ever the reason, the result is usually the same. The problem gets bigger and bigger and bigger. Before too long, conflict owns us and the relationship. Once this occurs conflict resolution seems like an overwhelming task. The smack, smack, smack of hammer upon nail rings in our ears as the lid starts to be sealed on yet another dead relationship. How unfortunate. If only we had kept short accounts.

Now let's see if we can apply all of this by coming full circle in this chapter. Consider how different the scenario between the troubled man and his pastor, at the beginning of the chapter, might have been if the man had repented of his selfish feelings and kept short accounts with his wife. Perhaps he would not even have spent that long evening with his pastor. Or what about the pastor? Once he lost it, how should he have handled the situation? Come the next morning, what course of action should he have chosen in order to follow the principles of Matthew 18:21-26? Step by step, it might look something like this:

Step #1: His first step would be to examine his feelings.

The pastor would need to repent. He would need to recognize that no matter how exasperated he might have been, blowing up was ultimately wrong. He would need to confess this to himself and to God.

Steps #2 and 3: His second and third steps would come together. He would seek quick reconciliation in order to maintain short accounts.

The pastor would need to confess his sin to the other man. A quick phone call to make an appointment would be in order. At the meeting, he would simply need to speak the truth. Focusing on his sin, he would need to refrain from any excuse based upon the other guy's attitude and/or behavior. A sincere apology, an admission of wrong, a confession of regret, and an appeal for forgiveness would all be in order.

Calvin Coolidge once said, "We cannot do everything at once, but we can do something at once." A willingness to care for problems quickly enables the obedient Christian to practice President Coolidge's advice. Ignoring our own responsibility or procrastinating on our responsibility defeats our opportunity to follow his advice.

Application

Reading Step

Please read through Matthew chapter five. Now read and reread verses 21-26 again.

Thinking Step

The Christian does not come to the altar in the same way the Jewish people to whom Jesus was speaking did. In fact we have no altar, because we have no temple made from mortar and brick. Yet, the response of the heart should be no different. When the Jewish person came to the altar he or she could come out of habit in an act of ritual or out of love in an act of worship. When Christians bow their hearts before God they can do so out of habit in acts of ritualism or out of love in acts of worship. Of course, we want the latter.

Added to this act of worship is the need for making our relationships right. This brings to light the fact that nothing we do is ever really private. All our decisions and actions impact someone other than ourselves. Too often we believe we can forget about how our choices have affected others and go on our merry way with God's forgiveness and blessing. However, God did not create us to be psychological in nature but sociological. We were never intended to be singular. In fact, in all the created beauty of those first seven days, God's first and only negative evaluation was "it is not good for man to be alone." We need one another.

Moving Out Step

So, is it possible that you are living with a hurting and sin-filled relationship for which you bear the primary responsibility. If so, let's put some reality—even some names—on the situation.

Who else feels the impact of this problem relationship:

Name:

_____

Name:

_____

Name:

_____

Now if this hurting relationship is going to be made right you will need to get moving. So how about writing yourself an action plan? Take it a step at a time. Use the following process to help you sort things out and turn a plan into action.

Grab a pen and some paper and...

A **Conflict Resolution Action Plan** for when I am responsible for creating problems in the relationship:

First: go back and review the commentary just offered on Matthew 5:21-26. Write out the salient features you need to remember and to which you need to respond.

Second: Detail a step by step action plan for seeking reconciliation in this relationship. Steps one through four are done for you. They are based on what you've learned in this chapter as well as earlier chapters. Step number five and the following are up to you. Decide what will be involved in your conflict resolution process. Will you ask anyone for advice? Will you talk over the phone? Will you set up a face to face appointment? If so, where will you meet? Etc.

#1
Begin with prayer: Chapter One
Review the principles: Chapter Two
Check your attitudes: Chapter Three

#2
Examine your feelings: Do you in fact need to repent?

#3
Seek reconciliation: You need to initiate healing.

Is there anything you need to do before contacting the other person?

Do you have the facts straight in your head?

Is anyone else involved?

If so, should they be included?

Are there any financial matters to be considered?

Are there any legal matters that need your attention?

Any other matters?

#4
Keep short accounts. You need to act promptly. You need to avoid procrastination.

#5

_____

_____

#6

_____

_____

#7

_____

_____

#8

_____

_____

#9

_____

_____

#10

_____

_____

A Second Method for Conflict Resolution

When Another Is Responsible for Conflict
Matthew 18:15-17

We all know full well the extent of hurt produced in people by the unkind words and deeds of others. It's long and deep. So, how heavenly would it be if wives could only be spared from the onslaught of insensitive and abusive husbands? How heavenly would it be if husbands could only be spared from the onslaught of insensitive and abusive wives? How heavenly would it be if only children could be spared the onslaught of domineering parents? Oh, if only...if only...

Someday, for those who know Jesus Christ, we will be spared the onslaught of the insensitivity and abusiveness of one another. That someday, however, is when we enter the Lord's presence.

Heaven will be glorious. One person described heaven as a place where parents can nap whenever they like and children never have to nap. Who knows, maybe this is why mythical pictures of heaven contain chubby cherubs relaxing on puffy clouds. Clouds do present themselves capable of sustaining both parents at rest and kids at play—at least in the paintings.

Of course, every student of the Bible knows heaven is not like this. Still, the seeds of truth are sometimes buried in wishful thinking. The Bible does, though not completely, describe heaven. Consider Revelation 21:1-6 (NIV):

Then I saw a new heaven and a new earth, for the first heaven and the first earth had passed away, and there was no longer any sea. I saw the Holy City, the new Jerusalem, coming down out of heaven from God, prepared as a bride beautifully dressed for her husband. And I heard a loud voice from the throne saying, "Now the dwelling of God is with men, and he will live with them. They will be his people, and God himself will be with them and be their God. He will wipe every tear from their eyes. There will be no more death or mourning or crying or pain, for the old order of things has passed away." He who was seated on the throne said, "I am making everything new!" Then he said, "Write this down, for these words are trustworthy and true." He said to me: "It is done. I am the Alpha and the Omega, the Beginning and the End. To him who is thirsty I will give to drink without cost from the spring of the water of life."

Think about it. God *will wipe every tear from their eyes.* As a result *there will be no more death or mourning or crying or pain* for the troubles of this world will have passed away. This is our hope. This is what we long to experience. Yet, so long as we remain on earth, we must also remember what Jesus said to the disciples in John 16:33: *I have told you these things, so that in me you may have peace. In this world you will have trouble. But take heart! I have overcome the world.* We look forward to a day of perfection. However, we live in days of trouble.

While we await that day of perfection we need the ability to work within this fallen world. Sometimes we need a very specific method for approaching and confronting

103

someone who sins against us. We need a method that has as its aim reconciliation. We need a biblical answer for the following question...

What do I do when another person is responsible for creating problems in a relationship?

Again let's look at what our Lord Jesus said concerning problems of this sort. In Matthew 18:15-20, we find his instructions for working out differences in the event that someone sins against us. Perhaps the best and quickest approach at understanding this brief passage is to see it phrase by phrase.

However, before that, we need some background. We first need to see how the passage fits within its larger context. The Gospel recorded by Matthew is primarily a presentation of Jesus Christ as the one, the only, and the true Messiah-King of Israel. Of course, by and large, the Jewish nation rejected this wonderful truth and in the process rejected Jesus. Chapters 11 and 12 of Matthew record the growing opposition demonstrated by the people and leaders of Israel toward Jesus. Chapters 13 through 16:12 record this opposition and rejection in its full manifestation. When we come to 16:13-20 we find Peter's great confession concerning Jesus Christ: *You are the Christ, the Son of the living God.* From this point on, through chapter 20, Matthew records the preparation for and the teaching of Christ's kingdom. On the following page you can see this chain of events section by section:

Preparation and Teaching for Christ's Kingdom in Matthew 16:13 – 20:34	
16:13-17	Jesus is the Messiah, the Son of God
16:18-20	Jesus would build his Church
16:21-26	Jesus would have to suffer and die
16:27—17:13	Jesus seen in his glory
17:14-21	Jesus' kingdom is greater than the Enemy's
17:22,23	Jesus will be betrayed, killed, and raised
17:24-27	Jesus said his disciples were sons of his kingdom
18:1-5	Jesus said the kingdom belongs to the humble
18:6-9	Jesus said sin has no place in his kingdom
18:10-14	Jesus said that every individual is important to God
18:15-20	Jesus taught on how to care for the sins of others
18:21-35	Jesus taught on the limitless aspect of forgiveness
19:1-12	Jesus taught about divorce
19:13-15	Jesus taught concerning the place of children
19:16-26	Jesus taught on the perils of wealth
19:27—20:16	Jesus taught that kingdom service will be rewarded
20:17-19	Jesus again mentioned his soon and coming death
20:20-28	Jesus said kingdom greatness comes from service
20:29-34	Jesus showed his authority by healing two blind men

It is within this context that we find our Lord's teaching on what to do when someone sins against us. The context is important for two reasons. The first is the simple recognition that his words apply to Christians. In the beginning of this section Jesus said, *on this rock I will build my church and the gates of Hades will not overcome it* (16:18). What follows are the preparation, plans and policies for his people. The second reason is this: we cannot divorce our Lord's teaching on conflict resolution from its immediate surroundings. While it is true that we should confront an individual who has sinned against us (18:15-20)...

we must remember that members of Christ's kingdom are to humble themselves like little children (18:1-5),

we must remember that we too are prone to sin (18:6-9),

we must remember that every individual is important to the Great Shepherd (18:10-14),

and we must remember that within Christ's kingdom forgiveness knows no limits (18:21-35).

We must, therefore, engage in reconciliation (loving confrontation) with all the right attitudes, all the right motives, and all the right behaviors. Reconciliation means just that—when we confront someone who has sinned against us we seek a loving solution, not revenge or final separation. When we confront someone who has sinned against us we must do so with a humble and contrite heart (18:1-5). When we need to confront someone who has sinned against us we must be careful since we too are prone to sin (18:6-9). When we confront someone who has sinned against us we must remember how precious this person is to God (18:10-14). When we confront someone who has sinned against us we must be willing to forgive and forgive and forgive (18:21-35).

With this behind us, let's look at Matthew 18:15-20 (NIV) step by step and phrase by phrase...

Step #1: Our first step is to <u>be sure about what we are about to do</u>.

That sounds simple enough, but as we shall soon see this means assuring ourselves of some key issues. Like...

A.   Does the nature of the relationship demand conflict resolution?

B.   Has the other person truly sinned or am I just ticked off about something I don't like?

C.   Am I prepared to go to the other person and actually have a safe conversation?

D.   Am I willing to keep this problem confined to the smallest circle of knowledge possible?

So, let's consider each of these questions more carefully by concentrating on our Lord's words and phrases...

A.   Does the nature of the relationship demand resolution? Is the person related well enough to me?

<u>If your brother</u>

The word *brother* implies (at the very least) some kind of personal relationship. We must assume the person in question is in some way related to us. Whether through family, friendship, business, church or something else, this person is in some way related. How we respond to those close to us will be different than those strange to us. In fact, the Apostle Paul in 1 Corinthians 5 tells us to leave the judgment of unbelievers up to God. So in some cases we must avoid confronting an offender altogether.

B.　　Has the other person truly sinned?

If your brother <u>sins against you</u>

The phrase *sins against you* is clear and to the point. The assumption is this: indeed someone has truly sinned. There are times when we feel wronged, but are in fact not. For instance, suppose someone has told us how overbearing we've become lately. Our feelings may be hurt. We may feel an estrangement toward this person. Yet, his or her words may have been not only accurate but delivered with compassion and concern. This person has not sinned. Consequently, we have nothing against this person. Instead our anger, bitterness or whatever we may be feeling towards him or her belongs to us alone— and we are therefore back to the question posed in our last chapter, "What do I do when I am responsible for creating problems in a relationship?"

C.　　Am I prepared to go to the other person?

If your brother sins against you <u>go and show him his fault</u>

Assuming we are on the right course our next step is to humbly (Matthew 18:1-5) confront our offender. We must actually go. This will be hard to be sure, but it must be done. If not, we will not right the relationship.

Having gone, we need to show the offender his fault. This requires we camp only upon the problem and possible solutions and not upon character assassination. To show him his fault means we expose the sin and convince the sinner of the sin. It does not mean we dump any of our emotional baggage on the person. We must, therefore, be prepared with facts rather than feelings. We need to articulate the problem rather than attack the person.

D.   Am I willing to keep this problem confined to the smallest circle of knowledge possible?

If your brother sins against you go and show him his fault just between the two of you. If he listens to you, you have won your brother over

Our hope is restoration, not revenge. We must, therefore, take the phrase *just between the two of you* seriously and make every effort to maintain confidentiality. Should we skip this step we will communicate a lack of faith, hope, and love for the other person. Privacy communicates all of these and more. It alerts and tells the other person the relationship is important. As we are able, we must keep the circle reduced to the offender and the offended.

Of further interest is the lack of numerical guidance for this step. Jesus does not say whether or not this step should occur only once. However, when one weighs the atmosphere of the surrounding context, it seems right to suggest this step of humble confrontation could be repeated several times. The desire for restoration would seem to be accompanied by grace not hard and fast rules.

If this loving confrontation succeeds the relationship will be mended. Jesus said, *If he listens to you, you have won your brother over.* This is the goal. Nothing less will do.

Step #2: Our second step, <u>if continued reconciliation is necessary, is to go with a witness.</u>

Of course, it would be simply great if all the above settled the whole issue. Unfortunately, that is not how it goes sometimes. If step one fails to gain resolution we may need to move to the next level. Moving to the next level includes two details…

A.   Sometimes people just do not listen.

but if he will not listen

There will be times when denial will mark the offender. He may reject our attempts at reconciliation. He may counter-attack with false accusations. He may rationalize the sinful behavior in question. He may refuse to listen. He may even resort to the silent treatment. He might choose to walk away from and out of the relationship.

When it becomes apparent that personal attempts at reconciliation are not going to work we must then move ahead. When we realize the offender has shut us off we must try something new.

B.   Sometimes we will need assistance.

but if he will not listen <u>take one or two others along,</u>
<u>so that "every matter may be established by the testimony</u>
<u>of two or three witnesses"</u>

When our loving and humble attempts fall on ears that will not hear or when the other person adds to the offense by including others in their sin, we are then forced to broaden the circle of knowledge. The inclusion of other witnesses provides three helpful strategies.

•   It insures the accuracy of our pronouncement: did the other person truly sin against us?

•   It also confirms the other person's rejection: is he indeed refusing to reconcile?

•   It may establish that we haven't enough support to continue this process: is it simply my word against the other person's?*

---

*The phrase *every matter may be established by the testimony of two or three witnesses* assumes others know there is a wrong. When the problem comes down to our word against another we cannot pursue this course. Instead, we will need to explore, "What do we do when responsibility is difficult to place?"

Hopefully, then, the assistance of these other witnesses will provide an atmosphere in which the wisdom of more heads then one might prevail. In this environment fairness to the accused can be assured and obedience to the word of God can be followed (Deut.19:15). These are vitally important if we are to remain true to Christ's desire that we remain humble, forgiving servants...not spiteful, vindictive victims. Witnesses are also important should we have to move beyond this point.

At some point, if the offender refuses even to listen to these combined efforts we might need to move on to the next step. However, before we do so, we need to remember the same caution that we applied back in Step #1: the number of times we attempt Step #2 (i.e. going with witnesses) is not carved in stone. Maybe once will tell us all we need to know. Maybe several times will be needed. And maybe, because the emotional and relational price may simply be too high if we proceed, we might choose to stop at this point. Whatever the case may be, humility, compassion, and love will help guide us toward a decision.

Step #3: Our third step is to <u>tell it to the church</u>.

if he refuses to listen to them, tell it to the church

If the sin is established by multiple witnesses and if the offender refuses to respond favorably to the party of witnesses, we may then need to broaden the circle of knowledge again. But why? Certainly this is not any kind of option one would want to pursue.

Why would we make this problem known to a larger group of people? What sort of advantage will this bring? The answer is found in verses 18-20: Jesus said, *I tell you the truth, whatever you bind on earth will be bound in heaven, and whatever you loose on earth will be loosed in heaven. Again, I tell you that if two of you on earth agree about anything you ask for, it will be done for you by my Father in heaven. For where two or three come together in my name, there I am with them.*

You see, the Church is heavenly. It is not simply a loose gathering of individuals. It was established by Jesus Christ. It is enabled by God the Father. It is always in the presence of the Holy Spirit. It is trans-cultural and trans-racial. It offers no merit based on age, sex, or social status. It's a bunch of equals at the foot of the cross.

So, again, hear what Jesus said: *for where two or three come together in my name, there I am with them.* The wisdom, the love, the care, the pressure and the hope of the church is greater than the wisdom, love, care, pressure and hope of an individual or of a few. When functioning properly within these parameters the church can be a mighty agent in the process of reconciliation.

While the circle of knowledge remains singular or small the loving confrontation remains singular and small. When we enlarge that circle of knowledge the loving confrontation is then also enlarged. The church can then combine its efforts. In fact, this will increase the love and care responses generated on this person's behalf in at least three areas:

- Prayer

More people will privately pray for the brother or sister who is in sin.

- Personal contact

More people will privately and lovingly exhort admonish, and encourage the one who is in sin.

- Persuasion.

More persuasive interaction will occur for the brother or sister who is in sin because of the private actions of a few more people.

The hope, of course, looks for repentance and restoration not stigma and separation. As God is patient, so we must be patient. We cannot be hasty before we move ahead. This step requires our willingness to wait. It requires us to be long-suffering If we are reluctant to wait we might ask ourselves, "How long is God willing to wait upon each of us?"

Two cautions are also in order.

A.   Enlarging the circle of knowledge is not a license to gossip.

Including others does not necessarily demand we include everyone. Should we feel that including every member of the church is what Jesus was calling for in this passage, we would also need to ask ourselves a question: "What is the logical conclusion of such thinking?" The logical conclusion, of course, would be all church members. This would not be limited to a local congregation since Jesus did not address the church like this in the Gospel of Matthew. The logical conclusion to this line of reasoning would, therefore, include believers near and far—many of whom the offender would not even know. In the end, this would be simply nothing more than just a very large exercise in gossip.

B.   Enlarging the circle does not require a formal, public meeting.

Nothing in this passage of Scripture states categorically that we should call together the entire church body in order to publicize these proceedings. Jesus did not ask that the sinning brother or sister be caused public ridicule and shame. His intention had nothing to do with some kind of tribunal. His goal was reconciliation. It certainly was not condemnation. In fact, nothing about the Savior would ever give us call to think otherwise.

Finally, then, if we choose to enlarge the circle, we need to be careful who is included in the circle. We need to choose people able to handle such a situation with great love and kindness. Their hope and goal must be the same as ours—reconciliation. They must be committed to the very best for everyone involved. They must be loyal to everyone involved. They must have the ability to go the distance with everyone involved. They must have the maturity to keep confidences. They must know the Bible well so they can give true biblical advice rather than opinions based on personal experience or pop-psychology. Finally, they must be quite well respected by everyone involved.

Step #4: Our fourth step is to <u>respond in love as you would to the lost</u>.

> *and if he refuses to listen even to the church,*
> *treat him as you would a pagan or a tax collector*

In the final analysis an unrepentant sinner is to be treated as though he or she was lost rather than saved. To treat him as you would a *pagan or a tax collector* is to treat the person as though there were no heaven-sent bond between the two of you. In Christ there should be a perfect bond of love and harmony (Colossians 3:14). This is a bond that surpasses the efforts and wisdom of our world. It is a bond that is missing between those who have received Jesus Christ and those who have not. Without such a bond the interaction between two people cannot help but be different than were the bond present.

Yet before we get ahead of ourselves we need to recall just how Jesus treated *pagans and tax collectors*. We may be surprised at what we find. Consider for instance the passage found in Mark 2:13-17 (NIV):

Once again Jesus went out beside the lake. A large crowd came to him, and he began to teach them. As he walked along, he saw Levi son of Alphaeus sitting at the tax collector's booth. "Follow me," Jesus told him, and

Levi got up and followed him. While Jesus was having dinner at Levi's house, many tax collectors and sinners were eating with him and his disciples, for there were many who followed him. When the teachers of the law who were Pharisees saw him eating with the sinners and tax collectors, they asked his disciples: "Why does he eat with tax collectors and sinners?" On hearing this, Jesus said to them, "It is not the healthy who need a doctor, but the sick. I have not come to call the righteous, but sinners."

Pagans, sinners, tax-collectors—to the Pharisees these were the scum of the earth. *Pagans* were not among the chosen. They were not Israeli. *Sinners* refused to abide by ritual and ceremony. They did not live up to the fine letter of the Pharisees rules. *Tax-collectors* were traitors. They worked for the enemy. In the eyes of Israel's first century leaders, folks like these were not fit to be around. Not so with Jesus.

Jesus did not refuse to interact with the lost. He gave them his time in abundance. It was the self-righteous religious folk (*Pharisees*) who had no time for the lost. Our part, naturally, is to follow Jesus and his example. Therefore, to treat someone like a *pagan* or a *tax-collector* does not mean we have absolutely nothing whatsoever to do with the individual. Instead, we must concentrate our efforts in different ways. The *pagan* and *tax-collector* had yet to acknowledge Jesus Christ as Savior. So they were not the recipients of his discipline, but his loving concern. The Bible tells us that God so loved the lost that he sacrificed his only Son for them.

117

The Father was willing. The Lord Jesus was willing. The only question left is, "Are we willing?" And, if we are, what exactly will this mean to us? It means that our conversation and interaction with the lost will take on certain nuances. For example:

• Our conversation among those who have not yet received Jesus Christ for salvation will be quite different than it is among the truly redeemed.

• We should expect less from those in which the Holy Spirit does not dwell. We do so because we realize the futility of laying conduct rules upon people not yet able to respond to God in obedience.

• A person treated as a *pagan and tax-collector* will not share as deeply in our fellowship as will believers.

• We will not allow the lost to teach.

• We will not allow the lost spiritual leadership.

• We will not allow the lost to share our difficult prayer burdens.

In general, then, the level of association is reduced—not by quantity, but by kind.

In personal relationships like these we might simply consider reducing our expectations of the other person. We may find it necessary to avoid "getting to the heart of the matter." We may need to be the one who "goes the extra mile." Of course, patience and long-suffering will become our calling-cards. We may also find ourselves a little more reluctant to share our deep feelings with the other person. And, since this will hurt indeed, we will need to find ourselves experiencing intimacy with Christ as never before.

Some might ask, "But isn't this saying that we know whether or not someone has truly received Jesus Christ or not? Who are we to stand in judgment over someone's eternal salvation?" These are very, very fair questions. However, this is not the case. Treating someone as though he is a *pagan and tax-collector* is not the same as passing judgment on his or her eternal condition. It is, instead, a response calculated to help the person see what his or her behavior and attitude looks like. Saved or not, the person who refuses to listen even to the church "looks" as though he or she is functioning without the presence of God. This person is acting as though he or she is in need of redemption.

So, while this individual undergoes a reduction of fellowship—by kind, not quantity—he or she should not be removed from our presence altogether. Would we turn our back on a lost neighbor should we chance to meet in the supermarket? Would we stand at the doors of our meeting places barring the lost any entrance? Do we fail to invite the lost into our homes? If we would or if we do then we have missed the very heart of the Savior's instructions. Jesus loved everyone, follower or not. Jesus died for everyone, obedient or not. It was Jesus who lamented for the hardened people of Jerusalem when he cried, *O Jerusalem, Jerusalem, the one who kills the prophets and stones those who are sent to her! How often I wanted to gather your children together, as a hen gathers her brood under her wings, but you were not willing!* Many were (and are) not willing. Jesus, on the other hand, gave up his life. That is love. That is going the distance. That is what we should do.

Our conversation with this individual will then, by necessity, be altered. How we go about this relationship will and must begin to look somewhat different. We may find ourselves saying things like, "I know that I am not perfect and you are perfectly free to confront me on my issues, but right now I just have to say what you are involved in is sin. Your refusal to repent looks as though you do not care. It looks like any possible connection to God is meaningless. Now because I love you and care for you, I can't help but remind you of how your actions are grieving the Savior."

It may not be an easy assignment, but it is a loving assignment. Anything less simply implies we do not care. Remember: When another is responsible for a breach in a the relationship...

Step #1: Be assured of the relationship: Is this person a brother? Be assured of the sin: Has this person truly sinned against you? Go to the offender and seek reconciliation. Keep the matter private: the circle of knowledge should always be kept to a minimum.

Step #2: Go with a witness.

Step #3: Tell it to the church.

Step #4: Respond in love as you would to the lost.

Application

Reading Step

Please read Matthew 18. Now please read verses 15-20 again. And again. And yet gain. Think while you read. Mull over the context. Look for relationships between ideas. Slow down. Pray. Read some more.

Thinking Step

Think for a moment what it would be like if you had never in your life encountered a difficult time. Go ahead.

What are the results of your thoughts? Are you saying "Wow, that would be great!?" Or, are you saying, "Yuck, that would be boring!?" In a way both would probably be accurate. It would be nice to sail through life with unbroken relationships, with never an unkind word, with rose petals and not thorns. On the other hand how would we then ever know the joy of victory after the agony of defeat? How would we learn about the sweet rest that comes after we endure loss, pain, suffering or even persecution if we never encountered some form of hardship? How would we ever be able to comfort others if we never really knew the sting of difficulty ourselves? How indeed?

The point is this: okay life sometimes hurts, but there is always hope. Despair is not the answer. It is especially not the answer when other people are involved (and they always are). If you are presently experiencing trauma in a relationship due to another's sin try practicing what you've just learned.

Moving Out Step

Is it possible that you are living with a hurting and sin-filled relationship in which someone else actually bears the responsibility. If so, let's once again put some names on the situation.

Who else feels the impact of this problem relationship?

Name:

_____

Name:

_____

Name:

_____

Now, as always, if this hurting relationship is going to be made right you will need to get moving. So, how about writing out your plans again? Take it a step at a time. Use the worksheet steps starting below to develop your strategy and tactics.

Once again, grab something to write on and...

A **Conflict Resolution Worksheet** for when another is responsible for creating problems in a relationship:

First: go back and briefly review the four steps of Matthew 18:15-20.

Second: Make a plan for seeking reconciliation in this relationship. Once again, the first several considerations have been prepared for you. #1 is based upon previous chapters. #2 through #5 correlate to this chapter. The rest are up to you. They should be based upon all that you have learned so far.

#1
Begin with prayer: Chapter One
Review the principles: Chapter Two
Check your attitudes: Chapter Three
Examine your feelings: Chapter Four

#2
Be assured of the relationship: Does it demand conflict resolution?

#3
Be assured of the sin: Did he or she actually sin or not?

#4
If two and three are affirmed, go privately to the offender.

How should this be handled? A simple phone call? A letter? Appointment? Formal setting? Informal setting? Your place? His or her place? Public place? Etc.

#5
Evaluate your first meeting. Was it successful? Will you need to go again? Will witnesses be needed?

#6

_____

_____

#7

_____

_____

#8

_____

_____

#9

_____

_____

#10

_____

_____

A Third Method for Conflict Resolution

When Responsibility for Conflict Is Difficult to Place
Colossians 3:12-17

There are times when problems erupt within relationships entirely disconnected from any one person's choices and/or responsibility. The old saying "It takes two to tango," is quite true. There are times when both parties— or, in the case of a group, many parties—are equally responsible for conflict within a relationship. At times like these we would do well to consider the truth of Philippians 2:3,4 (NIV) which states: *Do nothing out of selfish ambition or vain conceit, but in humility consider others better than yourselves. Each of you should look not only to your own interests, but also to the interests of others.* A quick reminder about Paul's letter to the Philippians will demonstrate how this brief passage relates to our subject matter. As you may recall from Philippians 1 and 2, Paul was concerned with the internal problems of the Philippian Church. Their relationships were important. One way to help them survive was through personal humility—the willingness to put aside one's own needs, feelings, desires, etc. for the well-being of the relationship. At times, we just need to be humble.

So, how do we go about this—especially when conflict seems to lack definition? What do we do when the finger of responsibility cannot be pointed at any one person or group? Paul answered this question in another letter. In his letter to the Church of Colosse, he developed several principles of true humility that help solve problems even when responsibility for the problem is difficult to place.

Open your Bible and read around and through Colossians 3:12-17 (remember, context is vital). In a section dealing with how to live our new lives with Jesus Christ as our leader, the word of God takes up the subject of how we should respond to one another even when there are grievances. The Apostle Paul had just finished telling the Colossians to put away those things which characterize people before knowing Christ (Col. 3:1-11). Then, in Colossians 3:12-17, he turned the discussion to those things which should characterize the person who has accepted Christ Jesus. What we find in this brief list of character qualities is a new standard for personal conduct within our relationships. Let's see just how these new character qualities can help us with our dilemma...

What do we do when responsibility for relational problems is difficult to place?

We'll find four practical steps in this passage of scripture that will help solve this riddle. Implementing any one of them will greatly help us resolve conflict. However, taken together, they form a complete and almost unbeatable package. Let's take a look at the first one…

Step #1: Our first step is to <u>take inventory of our own character</u> . 3:12

Therefore, as God's chosen people,
holy and dearly loved,

Before moving ahead, let's make the same assumption the Apostle Paul made: these instructions are for Christians. *God's chosen people, holy and dearly loved* can apply only to those truly redeemed. Therefore, his following instructions can only be fully appropriated by those who have accepted Jesus Christ as their Savior. Well, then, will those instructions apply to you?

If you are not sure please consider the following. There are four spiritual laws that govern our relationship with the Creator of the universe.

The first is this: God loves you and he has your best interests in mind. The Bible says, *For God so loved the world that he gave his one and only Son* (Jesus Christ)*, that whoever believes in him shall not perish but have eternal life* (John 3:16 NIV)). Jesus said, *The thief comes only to steal and kill and destroy; I have come that they may have life, and have it to the full* (John 10:10 NIV).

The second spiritual law is this: Man is utterly sinful and separated from God. Therefore, he cannot on his own know and experience God's love. The Bible says, *for all have sinned and fall short of the glory of God* (Romans 3:23 NIV). The Bible also says, *For the wages of sin is death, but the gift of God is eternal life in Christ Jesus our Lord* (Romans 6:23 NIV).

The third spiritual law is this: Jesus Christ is God's only answer for man's sin. We simply cannot remove the guilt of our sin on our own. However, through Christ we can see the guilt of our sin removed. The Bible says, *But God demonstrates his own love for us in this: While we were still sinners, Christ died for us* (Romans 5:8 NIV).

The fourth spiritual law is this: We must individually receive Jesus Christ as Savior and Lord so that we can know and experience God's love. Again, the Bible says, *Yet to all who received him* (Jesus Christ), *to those who believed in his name, he gave the right to become children of God* (John 1:12 NIV).

Question: Are you sure of your salvation? If not, would you like to receive Jesus Christ as your Lord and Savior? If so, simply express that desire to him. The following short prayer might be of assistance: "Lord Jesus, right now I choose to go your way. Thank you for giving your life for me. I accept your forgiveness for my sin. I ask you to come in and take over the control of my life. Thank you for your wonderful gift of eternal life. From now on, I want to follow you. Help me to study your word, the Bible. Help me to communicate with you through prayer. Help me to honor you and the Father and the Holy Spirit. And, again, thank you for accepting me into your family."

If this is the earnest cry of your heart be assured that God will not fail you. It is his great delight to enjoy fellowship with you. Welcome, then, to the family.

Let's return now to the Apostle Paul's instructions in Colossians 3:12…

Therefore, as God's chosen people, holy and dearly loved, <u>clothe yourselves with compassion, kindness, humility, gentleness and patience</u>

When we take inventory of our own character we need to double-check our emotional well-being. Can it be said of us that *compassion, kindness, humility, gentleness and patience* characterize our responses toward others in the midst of relational conflict? What about those times when personal responsibility for the problem cannot be placed? What if the problem seems to have no clear solution? Should we forget about it? Sweep it under the rug? No.

In times like these our responses must still be Christ-like. We need to initiate reconciliation without being overly concerned about the who, what, when and where of it all. A useful response during times like these might sound something like this: "You know, I'm not sure why this tension exists between us, but I do know that I consider our relationship more important than anything standing between us. Do you think we can solve this quickly...as soon as possible even?"

Compassion, kindness, humility, gentleness and patience spring from a soul well healed. They come forth when our love for others transcends problems and issues. When the question is "What do we do when responsibility cannot be placed," the answer must be "Don't worry too much about it." Instead, take a quick inventory of your character. Are the Christ-like qualities of *compassion, kindness, humility, gentleness and patience* alive and active in your makeup?

Step #2: Our second step is to <u>initiate the fruit of Christ-like character.</u> 3:13

Bear with each other and forgive whatever grievances
you may have against one another.
Forgive as the Lord forgave you.

When *compassion, kindness, humility, gentleness and patience* mark our character, forbearance and forgiveness will mark our behavior. Forbearance may be an old fashioned word. However, it is precisely what the Apostle meant when he said *bear with each other.* It is the ability to put up with others even while they themselves are unbearable. And, when Paul also said *forgive whatever grievances you may have against one another,* he had in mind the act of wiping the slate clean or returning the score to zero. Forbearance allows for the faults in others. Forgiveness let's others off the hook.

While we ponder these things we need also to realize the text does not demand contrition from the other person before we are encouraged to forbear and forgive. It is not absolutely necessary for the other person to reciprocate. We can forbear. We can forgive. We need not expect a similar reaction from the person or persons with whom we're experiencing difficulty.

During times of troubled confusion when it is not clear who is responsible for the conflict we simply need to take responsibility for our actions by initiating the fruit of Christ-like character. Again, notice the example we are to follow, *Forgive as the Lord forgave you.* How did the

Lord forgive us? Well Jesus, while hanging on the cross, said, *Father, forgive them, for they do not know what they are doing* (Luke 23:34). He was not the aggressor...he was not at fault...he didn't have to...still he forgave us.

Step #3: Our third step is to remain <u>motivated by sacrificial love</u>. 3:14

And over all these virtues put on love, which binds them all together in perfect unity

The Greek word used here for *love* is *agape*. It is the kind of love God has for us. It is a love that sacrifices much for the well-being of others. Some have called it unconditional love, but sacrificial love seems a better description. While it is clearly an act that accepts another freely, it demands much from the one loving. It gives up any thoughts of self-fulfillment and moves us toward other-centeredness. In cases where trouble exists within relationships it motivates an individual to do whatever is best for the other person or group. Where responsibility for conflict cannot be easily identified this kind of love spurs its possessor to create within him or herself *compassion, kindness, humility, gentleness and patience* leading to forbearance and forgiveness. This kind of love moves a person to look for solutions.

Step #4: Our fourth step is to <u>enact new strategies</u>. 3:15-17

As children of God we are now identified with him. We need to act accordingly. While in the heat of relational battle we need to stop long enough to develop some more strategies and tactics. In verses fifteen through seventeen, Paul offered four specific strategies that can help us shift our energy away from the emotions that accompany conflict to the needed skills that overcome conflict.

A.   Let's long for peace, not tension.

Let the peace of Christ rule in your hearts,
since as members of one body you were called to peace

When conflict arises, we might ask ourselves, "Is the *peace of Christ* ruling in my life right now?" If the answer is "No," we need to stop long enough to pray our way back. The only way to maintain peace at the core of who we are is to constantly meditate upon the good things we receive from God. By "the good things we receive from God" we do not necessarily mean material items. Consider the goodness of God in providing for our eternal salvation. Think of the awesome implications of having God, the Holy Spirit, active in our lives. Or what about those everyday miracles like breath and sleep? See, when a person gets serious about thanking God, peace will begin to flow. Instead of envy or spite toward what others have or do, we maintain mercy and love toward them, because our greatest needs are met in Christ.

B.   Let's be thankful, not spiteful.

Let the peace of Christ rule in your hearts,
since as members of one body you were called to peace.
<u>*And be thankful.*</u>

Can you imagine it? Faces are red with anger. Eyes are popping with tension. Veins in the neck are at an all-time high. Two people or a group of people are in the middle of deep conflict. Suddenly, someone says, "Can we stop and thank God for the good things we share? Can we pause long enough to thank one another for all the wonderful times we've shared? Can we be thankful that we care enough about one another that we view this problem with such intensity?" One wonders what might happen to the conflict then.

C.   Let's search the Bible, not argue.

Let the peace of Christ rule in your hearts, since as members of one body you were called to peace. And be thankful. <u>Let the word of Christ dwell in you richly as you teach and admonish one another with all wisdom, and as you sing psalms, hymns and spiritual songs with gratitude in your hearts to God.</u>

Again, it is difficult to see how tension, conflict, anger, resentment and the like can continue while the children of God sincerely follow a strategy like this. Consider the husband and wife who find themselves on the edge of verbal terrorism. They have learned the warning signs. They know the trench they are about to fall into. They've been here before. So they look deep into one another's eyes. They suddenly realize they are no longer even sure what prompted the conflict. They then begin to practice what they know is truth for troubled hearts. One or the other sounds the retreat. Compassion, kindness, humility, gentleness and patience quickly produce forbearance and forgiveness. Godly love then motivates one or the other to pray: "O God, is not our relationship greater than this problem?" And, then, like a gentle breeze on a muggy night, he or she says to the other, "Let's double-check God's word. Maybe we'll find the answer we need."

Sounds mighty idealistic, doesn't it? Perhaps. Yet, that is what Paul called us to when he wrote *Let the word of Christ dwell in you richly*. Faithful students of the Bible hide God's truth in their hearts. When the time comes, the Holy Spirit will bring it to mind. The power of the Bible is not lost in its pages, but in our lack of searching its pages. However, we can take it a step further. We can actually look for biblical answers as an active tactic for resolving conflict. Unresolved conflict would be a less probable occurance were people boardering on argument disciplined enough to search the Bible for answers to their problems.

Two things will come from this strategy. First, the very act of reading the Bible will cool the flare of conflict. One might refer to it as godly misdirection. By focusing on the Bible, we divert our energy away from emotional turmoil. That's a pretty good diversion. Second, we may find a specific biblical answer for the problem we face. If not a specific answer, we will find principles that apply to our problems. In both cases, the very act of looking into God's word will help to build the relationship.

Before going on to the next strategy, a word of warning about this strategy is greatly needed. This strategy can only work when each of the parties involved in conflict is willing to search the Bible. Each person needs to invest in the process with Christ-like character. Here's why…

There are times when one person uses his or her ability to "Study the Bible" as a sledge hammer. In these cases, the person with a so called biblical background chooses to access certain Bible passages to prove a point. It is not done with love. It is not done with compassion, kindness, humility, gentleness or patience. This is an abuse. It results in a twisted perversion of an otherwise healthy and ordained activity. Instead of looking for truth, this process looks for ammunition. Rather than searching for solutions to a problem, this process enables the abuser to proudly say, "I told you so." This has nothing to do with the Christ-like ministry of warning or rebuking with sympathy and love and everything to do with the self-centered preoccupation with condemning and hurting through power and control.

D.   Let's glorify Christ, not sin.

Let the peace of Christ rule in your hearts, since as members of one body you were called to peace. And be thankful. Let the word of Christ dwell in you richly as you teach and admonish one another with all wisdom, and as you sing psalms, hymns and spiritual songs with gratitude in your hearts to God. <u>And whatever you do, whether in word or deed, do it all in the name of the Lord Jesus, giving thanks to God the Father through him</u>

Whatever you do? In word or deed? In everything give thanks to God? Yes, so let's ask a few questions:

- "Is what I am about to say or do going to give glory to my Savior?"

- "Can I truthfully say my words and/or actions are being done *in the name of the Lord Jesus?*"

- "Am I *giving thanks to God the Father* or am I throwing everything to the wind without care for where it lands or who it hurts?"

Remember, Paul wrote *whatever you do, whether in word or deed, do it all in the name of the Lord Jesus, giving thanks to God the Father through him.* If this is true for us then we can answer "Yes" to the above questions. If not, "No" must be the answer. This obviously presents some problems and a need for confession. Horizontal conflict will likely never be resolved with any vertical conflict present.

We can also use questions like these very strategically in the middle of conflict situations. For example, if and when we decide to deliberately pause long enough to ask these questions in the middle of conflict, then and only then will we be truly shifting our attention away from our own egos to what is best for the relationship. Here's how it works:

- We dedicate ourselves to glorifying Jesus Christ in our lives.

- When faced with real conflict we remember our dedication to him.

•   So, we ask ourselves, "Does what I'm thinking bring God glory? Is what I am about to say or do going to give glory to my Savior? Will others think more highly of God on account of my words and deeds?"

•   This process allows us to disable our selfish inclinations and actions.

•   As a result, the relational issue of solving the problem takes precedence over the personal issue of winning the argument.

Now, as we begin to conclude this chapter, we need to emphasize that putting these steps and strategies together will indeed work. The major question should not be, "Who would ever stop to do these things in the middle of a conflict?" Rather, we should ask "Am I willing to follow God's word by enacting these strategies whenever I find myself in the middle of conflict?"

Remember: When responsibility for relational problems is difficult to place...

Step #1: Let's take inventory of our own character.

Step #2: Let's initiate the fruit of Christ-like character.

Step #3: Let's be motivated by sacrificial love.

Step #4: Let's enact new strategies...

        A.   Let's long for peace, not tension.

B.   Let's be thankful, not spiteful.

C.   Let's search the Bible, not argue.

D.   Let's glorify Christ, not sin.

Application

Reading Step

Please read Paul's letter to the Colossians. Now read Colossians 3 again. Now read verses 12-17 several more times. And, just as recommended in the last chapter's application section, "think while you read; mull over the context; look for relationships between ideas; slow down; pray; and read some more."

Thinking Step

Had you ever considered that methods for working out differences could differ so much depending upon where the responsibility fell? Does it make sense now?

Now let's shift our focus for a few moments. Do you suppose there are some problems and differences lying between you and someone else because you just don't know who is responsible? Is it possible that you are living with a hurting and sin-filled relationship simply because you and the other person do not know how to utilize the methods found in this chapter? If so, let's once again put some names on the situation.

Moving Out Step

Who else feels the impact of this problem relationship? Is it just one other person? Are there several people involved? List below the names of those who you need to resolve conflict with in this situation.

Name:

_____

Name:

_____

Name:

_____

Now, just like before, if this is something you are currently working on, you will need to get moving. So, how about writing yourself the game plan? Take it a step at a time. Use the following process to help you sort that game plan out.

A **Conflict Resolution Worksheet** for when the actual responsibility for relational problems is difficult to place:

First: go back and review the commentary just offered on Colossians 3:12-18.

Second: As in the last two chapters, make a plan for seeking reconciliation in this hurting relationship. Once again, the first considerations have been prepared for you. #1 is based upon previous chapters. #2 through #5 correlate to this chapter. The rest are up to you. They should be based upon what you have just learned from this chapter.

#1
Begin with prayer: Chapter One
Review the principles: Chapter Two
Check your attitudes: Chapter Three
Examine your feelings: Chapter Four
Be assured of the relationship: does it demand conflict resolution: Chapter Five

#2
Take inventory of your own character.

#3
Initiate the fruit of Christ-like character.

#4
Be motivated by sacrificial love.

#5
Enact new strategies…

> Long for peace, not tension.
>
> Be thankful, not spiteful.
>
> Search the Bible, not argue.
>
> Glorify Christ, not sin.

#6

_____

_____

#7

_____

_____

#8

_____

_____

#9

_____

_____

#10

_____

_____

The Art of Conflict Resolution

From the Apostle Paul's Letter
Concerning the Church: Ephesians

Webster's Dictionary, in part, defines the word "art" with this: "skill in performance acquired by experience, study, or observation." Art is more than simple know-how. Art involves precision. It demands the fine touch. So does conflict resolution.

In fact, the quality and speed of conflict resolution will usually depend upon just how much of the fine touch we can bring to the process. Should we stumble our way through the process—using poor choices and heated emotions—we're liable to make little progress. However, should we negotiate our way through the process—with art and precision—we stand a good chance of producing a quality resolution.

Of course, the art of conflict resolution will likely be demonstrated most in the act of communication. What we say, when we say it, and how we say it are of vital importance. It simply cannot be stressed enough, skilled communication—and thus, skilled conflict resolution—requires more than eagerness. It requires a fine touch. It requires more than verbal overload. It requires finesse.

Consider for a moment an example. Suppose John comes home late for the fifth day in a row. His mom and dad are, quite reasonably, upset. They are worried. They are a little angry. They are confused. They know who John has been hanging out with, but they've not been able to prevent it. Tonight is the final straw. There will indeed be confrontation. Dad figures these are the facts, the truth:

1.   John's the son, Mom and Dad the parents.

2.   Parents set the rules, not children.

3.   John is rebelling, that's sinful.

4.   Parents are supposed to do something for their children when they go over rebellion hill.

5.   The Bible says this, *Therefore each of you must put off falsehood and speak truthfully to his neighbor, for we are members of one body.*

6.   Tonight John will hear the truth and the meaning behind the truth (boy, will he ever)!

Now John is entering the front door. Dad meets him with the truth. The loud, red in the face, yelling sort of truth.

"Where in the world have you been? Who do you think you are? Don't you know you're still a child? What is the meaning of all this? We're your parents. You're supposed to obey us. The Bible says so. How long is this going to go on? Will you ever learn?!!"

Everything Dad said dealt with the truth. The problem did not lie so much in what he said, but in how he said it. His intense approach exploded in his son's face. Any hope for communication suffered the sting of verbal shrapnel. This was not skillful conflict resolution. It was hurtful. We might sympathize with Dad's anxiety regarding his son, but we must not sympathize with his approach.

What, then, is the art of conflict resolution? Much of it we have already seen wrapped within the packages of prayer, principles, attitudes, and methods. Still, there is more. In Paul's letter to the Ephesians, we find a well crafted section on what simply can be called "New Speech for New People." It's found in Ephesians 4:25-32.

Paul, addressing Christians, wrote this letter as a treatise on the Church, the Body of Christ. From before the foundations of the world God had chosen the Church (Ephesians 1). From Jew and Gentile alike, God chose to adopt lost people into his family (Ephesians 2). Paul's letter to the Ephesians tells us a great deal about this wonderful phenomenon. A portion of the letter tells us that as children of God, as members of the Church, we are to be different than others. Leading up to the passage we want to consider, Paul wrote, *So I tell you this, and insist on it in the Lord, that you must no longer live as the Gentiles do, in the futility of their thinking. They are darkened in their understanding and separated from the life of God because of the ignorance that is in them due to the hardening of their hearts. Having lost all sensitivity, they have given themselves over to sensuality so as to indulge in every kind of impurity, with a continual lust for more* (Eph. 4:17-19 NIV). As new people in Christ, Christians live by new standards. Again, the Apostle:

You, however, did not come to know Christ that way. Surely you heard of him and were taught in him in accordance with the truth that is in Jesus. You were taught, with regard to your former way of life, to put off your old self, which is being corrupted by its deceitful desires; to be made new in the attitude of your minds; and to put on the new self, created to be like God in true righteousness and holiness (Eph. 4:20-24 NIV). Much of this *true righteousness and holiness* involves the art of communication in working out our differences. Where it does not exist there is pain.

Observe...

There are churches where people do not know the art of conflict resolution. So: some members rule with loud voices; people are therefore afraid of change; embittered, they gossip and slander; eventually, the gospel is pushed aside; the problems are paramount—never solved, they will always sap the energy and life of the church. It is a shame…literally, a shame.

Observe...

There are families where people do not know the art of conflict resolution. So: sins are hidden; children endure abuse; parents separate; loneliness pervades; bitterness takes root; emotional and spiritual health disappears; and the cycle repeats itself in the next generation. A shame.

However, none of this is necessary. If we simply utilized all that we have learned so far we would be lightyears ahead of these sort of problems, but we are not finished. We have this one last passage of Scripture (Ephesians 4:25-32 NIV) to explore. In it we will find that…

The art of working out our differences involves the finesse and precision of well-crafted communication.

As we shall see, Ephesians 4:25-32 opens the door to a greater understanding of just how to go about the delicate task of communication. The Apostle Paul gives us six simple, yet brilliant, principles about communication that will help us develop an artistic flair for working out our differences as we pursue peace.

Item #1: Well-crafted communication must always be truthful and honest.

Therefore each of you must put off falsehood and speak truthfully to his neighbor… 4:25a

Why? Deceit destroys relationships.

…for we are all members of one body. 4:25b

Primary in the art of working out our differences is the need for honest and truthful communication. When we fail to relate to one another with honesty and truthfulness, we begin the steady erosion of a thing called trust. When trust begins to disappear, relationships start to fade. This is Paul's point about speaking truthfully. If we are members of *one body* (the Body of Christ, the Church), then we belong together. We need one another. Our relationships are necessary for the survival of the one and of the whole. Deception and falsehood always erode relationships. The inevitable break up is on the way.

So, what exactly is the contrast between falsehood and truthfulness? Falsehood involves deceit, lies, and, even, the old game "what they don't know won't hurt them." Truthfulness respects the importance of the other person. Truthfulness recognizes that each person is part of a whole. Deceiving one injures many—including oneself. Being truthful and honest involves a willingness to be open and transparent. It means we are willing to discuss tough issues. It means we help one another, we don't hinder one another.

Item #2: Well-crafted communication must be delivered with emotional self-control.

"In your anger do not sin": Do not let the sun go down while you are still angry... 4:26

Why? Satan will always use emotional panic to sieze an advantage.

...and do not give the devil a foothold. 4:27

Notice Paul did not say, "Never be angry." He said, *In your anger do not sin.* Anger is not always wrong. There are times when we feel anger due to provocation. This feeling in and of itself need not be sin or even become sin. What we need to learn is the art of managing anger. We need to learn how to bring it under the influence of

God. In doing so, we will learn to express anger properly. We do this by controlling our emotions.

Some will say, "This is hypocritical. To act one way and feel another is denying the true self." So says the wisdom of modern psychology. However, think about it for a moment. Push this foolishness to its logical conclusion. The thief feels like stealing so he steals. The mugger feels like mugging so he does. The gossip feels like spreading rumors so he blabs. We would never condone such actions. Why then do we allow the world to tell us it's okay to express ourselves just the way we're feeling? It makes no sense.

Two more issues scream for attention here. Here's the first issue: Why must communication be delivered with emotional self-control? The answer is that Satan uses our emotions to his advantage. Paul said, *Be angry, yet don't sin with your anger...and do not give the devil a foothold.* Seldom does conflict emerge simply due to differences of opinion. During the next argument you see or partake in, observe carefully the escalation of tempers. The tempers usually grow out of control after someone's voice has become edgy. One or another person will soon raise the level of their voice ever so slightly. This is matched by an equal or greater response by his or her opponent. Soon, conversation becomes argument. Argument then becomes conflict. Conflict then becomes a fight. Fighting becomes entrenched. Lines are drawn. Catastrophic failure nears.

This is the result of emotions, not issues. Now, please do not get this wrong. We're not saying emotions are bad.

Emotions are normal and natural. Yet, all mature people learn to control their emotions and invest them wisely.

Satan, on the other hand, wants to pervert our emotional make-up. Anger, bitterness, resentment, hostility, and the like, grown out of control give Satan the perfect platform for gaining a *foothold.*

The other issue is revealed with another question: "What does Paul mean by, *Do not let the sun go down while you are still angry?*" He means simply this: always keep short accounts with your anger. Rather than letting the day slip away, take care of the problem. The person who would develop the art of conflict resolution will acquire two talents: (1) short accounts with God—praying through problems every day; and, (2) short accounts with people—working through problems before they become out-of-control monsters.

Item #3: Well-crafted communication must always be constructive and helpful.

> *Do not let any unwholesome talk come out of your mouths,* 4:29a

Why? Constructive and helpful communication will always help others, but destructive communication will always hurt them.

> *but only what is helpful for building others up according to their needs, that it may benefit those who listen.* 4:29bc

Unwholesome talk is speech that tears others down. The adjective, *unwholesome*, means "rotton." We gather from this meaning the implication of worthlessness. This kind of communication is harmful, hurtful, destructive, and unkind. It never, never helps and instead it often, far too often, endangers.

- We do this when we harp on the negative.

- We do this when we nit-pick a situation as though letting it go is some kind of federal offense.

- We do this when we major on minor points (i.e. Sally said, "I got a ticket doing 45 miles per our." Her husband responds, "That was 47 miles per hour.").

- We do this when we over-expose the deficiencies of another.

- We do this when we attack, impune, and malign the character of another.

- We do this when we use intense and loud volume to outshout another.

- We do this when we begin to utilize silence as one of the weapons in our arsenal.

The question we must ask ourselves is this, "Do we want solutions for our problems or do we want to go on hurting one another with verbal and non-verbal communication?" If it's the former, we must avoid speech, gestures, voice tones, and expressive "looks" that relate hate, dislike, contempt, disgust, resentment, bitterness and the like.

The conflict resolution artist will avoid these like the plague. Instead, he or she will say only that which *is helpful for building others up according to their needs, that it may benefit those who listen.* The meaning here involves more than good speech. It is more than simply avoiding all that is negative or hurtful. It involves using communication that imparts "grace" or a benefit to the listener. So, while many will nudge by in working out differences, the person who desires to go a step further— the communication artist—will make every attempt to build up everyone involved.

The old saying, "Think, before you speak," is very appropriate here. In fact, elsewhere in the Bible we read this, *A man finds joy in giving an apt reply—and how good is a timely word* (Proverbs 15:23 NIV). Helpful communication travels on words spoken with skill—in the right fashion, at the right time, with the right intentions, relating the right ideas.

Item #4: Well-crafted communication will always be influenced by our desire to please God.

And do not grieve the Holy Spirit of God 4:30a

Why? Everything good we owe to him.

with whom you were sealed for the day of redemption.
4:30b

Wow! Christians are *sealed for the day of redemption*! The Holy Spirit of God assures us that our eternal life and heavenly inheritance remain forever secure. Whatever we face—no matter how tough or complicated—we can face it with the knowledge that God cares for us. Today may be filled with conflict, but the future looks very clear. This truth should make us grateful. And this gratitude should cause us to wish that God would be well-pleased with our attitudes and actions. Were this ever foremost in our thoughts, our ability to communicate in love would greatly increase. Think of it for a moment...

> "George, for crying-out-loud, how many times have I asked you not to leave your socks lying in the hallway!? What do you think I am, your slave? No, I'm your wife! Though, it seems I'm the only one who knows it. The way you act, you would think I was the invisible woman or something! George, when are you gonna get the big picture?"

How would you respond to this kind of verbal explosion? Of course, your answer depends on many factors: your personality, your maturity, your knowledge, your desires, etc. Yet, it's safe to say, most people would react. They would not respond with forethought. The "reactive" person speaks first, thinks later. It almost always makes things worse. What we need in situations like these is a "proactive" response. The proactive person thinks first, then speaks. What if we thought something like this: "Boy, Mary is really upset. What can I say that will not grieve God and will benefit Mary? Seriously, I need to be careful here."

> "Mary, I'm sorry. I do realize how much keeping the house in order is important to you. Please believe me, my laziness doesn't mean that I don't appreciate you. In fact, my inadequacies say nothing at all about you. They only reveal my limits. I'll try to do better. Will you forgive me?"

One can only imagine Mary's face.

Sure, we've created this scenario in the over-simplistic and sterile setting of paper and ink. Yet, we all know how close it strikes to reality. All of us also know that when we try to please God, we usually do that which pleases others as well. Therefore, the very attitude that frees us not to grieve the Holy Spirit will refine in us the art of conflict resolution.

Item #5: Well-crafted communication must never be violent or abusive.

Get rid of all bitterness, rage and anger, brawling and slander, along with every form of malice. 4:31

Notice how carefully Paul put this sentence together. From *bitterness* to *malice*, with *rage, anger, brawling, and slander* in between. It happens like this:

We fail to forgive. Resentment develops. And then…

- *Bitterness* toward another takes root.

- *Rage* produces calculated retaliation.

- *Anger* with no brakes creates passionate tantrums.

- *Brawling* then ignites—controversy, clamour and constant cackling mark our attitudes and actions.

- S*lander* (blasphemy and speaking evil) then begins to flow from our lips as we withdraw from others.

- *Malice* finally colors and covers our character. The product is anger gone underground. Everything we do and/or say from then on is under its evil influence.

If this is already a part of you then ask God for help. Specifically, look to gain all you have been learning.

Item #6: Well-crafted communication must always be influenced by a desire to be Christlike.

> *Be kind and compassionate to one another,*
> *forgiving each other* 4:32 a,b

Why? We have received from Jesus far more than we can ever give to others.

> *just as in Christ God forgave you.* 4:32c

Consider our Lord Jesus. Kindness and compassion were his calling cards. His love for mankind produced actions that can only be described as kind and compassionate. He touched and healed the man with leprosy—forbidden and taboo was such an action. He ate with the sinners and tax-collectors—forbidden and taboo again. He kept company with commoners and prostitutes—forbidden and taboo. He was and is magnificent. His kindness and compassion knew no limits.

It is precisely this kind of character we need to possess if we truly desire to develop the fine art of working out our differences. If we need a reason, we should look no further than verse 32 itself. God has forgiven us in Christ. Apart from the Savior, we were on our way to hell. Hell was not God's choice, but ours. The Bible says, *For God did not send his Son into the world to condemn the world, but to save the world through him. Whoever believes in him is not condemned, but whoever does not believe stands condemned already because he has not believed in the name of God's one and only Son* (John 3:17,18 NIV). By the grace of God, we've been given a second chance. Can we not also give others a second chance?

Remember:

Be honest—yes.
Control your emotions—absolutely.
Benefit the other—indeed.
Please God—for sure.
Never be abusive—of course.
Be Christ-like—it works.

This is the art of working out our differences.

Application

Reading Step

Please read Paul's letter to the Ephesians. Now please read Ephesians 4 again. Read verses 25-32 several times.

Thinking Step

Compare what you have just learned with the following two sets of Proverbs:

Group A:

10:18	*He who conceals his hatred has lying lips, and whoever spreads slander is a fool.*
12:16a	*A fool shows his annoyance at once...*
14:29b	*...but a quick-tempered man displays folly.*
15:1b	*...but a harsh word stirs up anger.*
15:2b	*...but the mouth of the fool gushes folly.*
15:18a	*A hot-tempered man stirs up dissension...*
18:13	*He who answers before listening—that is his folly and his shame.*
19:5	*A false witness will not go unpunished, and he who pours out lies will not go free.*

Group B:

12:16b   *...but a prudent man overlooks an insult.*

14:29a   *A patient man has great understanding...*

15:1a   *A gentle answer turns away wrath...*

15:2a   *The tongue of the wise commends knowledge...*

15:18b   *...but a patient man calms a quarrel.*

25:12   *Like an earring of gold or an ornament of fine gold is a wise man's rebuke to a listening ear.*

Answer this question: "Which group of Proverbs best descibes me right now: Group A or Group B?"

Moving Out Step

If your answer is Group A, there is work to be done. Try reading the following passages: Romans 12:1,2; James 1:21-27; 3:1-18; 5:16; and 1 John 1:5-2:1. Now take two more steps: the first is easy, the second not so easy.

1.   Write down the Proverbs from Group B on three by five cards and put them to memory.

2.   Take your findings to a trusted brother or sister in Christ. Share with him or her what you have learned. Ask

this person to be your Prayer Partner as you negotiate growth in this area of your life. Allow this person the opportunity and privilege of providing you with loving accountability. Meet together weekly. Practice diligently what you learn. Pray diligently about your needs.

Final Words

From the heart of Jesus:

Jesus said, A new command I give you: love one another.
As I have loved you, so you must love one another.
By this all men will know that you are my disciples,
if you love one another.

John 13:34,35

When the season is over, only the champions dance.

When the curtain falls, standing ovations occur when the actors have done well.

When the meal is finished the proof is in the pudding.

When the teacher let's the students out, the posting of passing grades allows everyone to sigh with relief.

When the world looks upon the Church, disciples of Christ Jesus are known by their love for one another...or not. The conclusion is simple: a desire to know Jesus and to make him known should motivate us to resolve our differences in love. Making this happen requires us to learn sound biblical principles, cultivate godly biblical attitudes, follow detailed biblical methods, and refine the biblical art of working out our differences. Failing to do so will severely limit our ability to let one person or the entire world know that we are followers of Jesus. And that is something much more than unfortunate.

Four final suggestions may prove helpful:

1.   Involve your volition. Resolve, will, determine to accomplish godliness. Make it your passion to do what is right. Let nothing keep you from this endeavor.

2.   Involve your intellect. Continue to study and to apply the Bible on this subject. Know the truth. Know it well. Live it.

3.   Involve your social network. Talk with others about these truths. Consider their thoughts. Cultivate a desire within your family, friends, church, business, and other organzations to allow love the honor of overcoming conflict and strife.

4.   Involve your spirit. Depend upon God for the strength to accomplish the first three. Pray without ceasing. Worship without end. Cultivate your love for our Savior. Walk with and be lead by the Holy Spirit. Acknowledge the sovereignty of God the Father. Do everything for the glory of God.

About Sound Communication

Jesus said fields all across the world are ready for the harvest. It comes as no surprise that he wants as many as possible to hear his message. At Sound Communication, we can think of no greater privilege than being a part of a team that delivers that message.

Since the first century, followers of Christ have dedicated themselves to this task. The times in which we live are no different. Faithful messengers still proclaim God's life-changing message of salvation through Jesus Christ. Ricki Lee Brooks is one of them.

Ricki's goal has always been to be not only motivational, but inspirational. Inspiring others to face and overcome hardship by developing their love for and connection with the Savior remains at the heart of all that he does. In fact, over thirty years ago, Ricki and his wife, Vanita, wrote down their mission statement for life. Here it is...

"Our mission in life is to love our Lord, one another, and our children more and more every day and to help as many as possible to do the same thing."

Since the loss of his beloved at the hands of a drunk driver, Ricki has often said, "Without her I feel less effective, but not less impassioned. Helping people love the Lord is the greatest privilege on earth, because, in the end, our purpose was never just about us...it was and is all about Jesus."

At Sound Communication we want to assist you with the skills you need to meet your unique challenges. We also want to give you a three-fold promise. First, should we accept the mission of assisting you, we will give you the absolute best of all we are and all we have to offer. Second, we will not offer what we cannot reasonably accomplish. Therefore, you can always count on us for an honest assessment of both your dilemma and our "fit" on behalf of your dilemma. Third, anything you can purchase from Sound Communication in hard-copy you can also download for free.

So, if and when you have the opportunity, visit Ricki's website or make a call.

Sound Communication

A Division of West Sound Community Church
PO Box 4016
Silverdale, WA 98383

360.362.6686   360.779.9996

rickileebrooks.com
ricki@westsound.org

Made in the USA
Monee, IL
21 October 2020

45297810R00095